RAGTIME RARITIES

Complete Original Music for 63 Piano Rags

Selected and with an Introduction by
TREBOR JAY TICHENOR

Dover Publications, Inc., New York

Publisher's Note

Since the originals reproduced here are faithful historical documents as well as sources of enjoyment, the titles, textual material and artwork have not been changed even where they reflect the broader humor of their era, in which the nation was far less sensitive to jibes about minority groups. It is our belief that a mature understanding of our past is more fruitful than a falsification of history.

Acknowledgments

Much of the following ragtime lore is gratefully borrowed from *They All Played Ragtime* by Rudi Blesh and Harriet Janis (Quick-Fox, Inc., New York), the ragtimers' "bible."

Such an in-depth compilation of rags as the present volume is possible only through the enthusiastic cooperation of fellow collectors and historians. I would like to thank the following friends for their help: Mike Montgomery, Thornton Hagert, Dave Jasen, Harold and Thelma Doerr, Alice and Dewey Green, Elliott Adams, Ed Sprankle, Tex Wyndham and The Ragtime Society of Canada, Dick Zimmerman of The Maple Leaf Club, Bob Wright, Bob Ault, Eric Sager, Albert Mothershead of the St. Louis Ragtime Guild, Mike Schwimmer, William Robertson, Al Rose, Bob Darch, Roger C. Hankins, and my own St. Louis Ragtimers.

Ragtime Rarities: Complete Original Music for 63 Piano Rags is a new collection of music, selected and with an introduction by Trebor Jay Tichenor, first published by Dover Publications, Inc., in 1975. The original publishers and dates of publication of the music appear in the Contents and on the individual covers and title pages.

International Standard Book Number: 0-486-23157-7
Library of Congress Catalog Card Number: 74-28941

Manufactured in the United States of America
Dover Publications, Inc.
180 Varick Street
New York, N.Y. 10014

INTRODUCTION

The 1890's were a time of musical revolution in America: a new sound called ragtime burst upon the scene, displacing the maudlin sentimentality, the pallid importations of the Victorian era—syncopation now ruled the nation. Ragtime had a freshness, a power and conception that belied a rather haphazard development out of a complex nineteenth-century musical ferment. And the threads may never be completely unraveled—the phonograph came too late for us to hear how it happened. But there is no doubt that the rag has Afro-American folk roots; while the true sounds of older black music are forever lost—the juba dances, plantation fiddles and banjos—the spirit is reflected in the popular music of the blackface minstrels of that day. The seeds of our native music were sown here in such tunes as "Old Dan Tucker" and "Zip Coon," as imported music traditions became enriched with an amalgam of folk elements, both black and white.

The hallmark of this transformation was a restless energy, a brash optimism that was expressed through syncopation. At some point lost to memory the idea of a consistently syncopated melodic line played against a regular-metered march bass was tried out on the piano. The place of origin was the "underground"—the saloons and pleasure emporiums of the late nineteenth century where itinerant black pianists transformed the old marches, quadrilles and schottisches into syncopation. Keyboard instruments had been generally inaccessible to black people before the Civil War, and were much sought after later. Many of the pioneers, including Eubie Blake, began by ragging familiar tunes on the family reed organ— usually inspiring parental ire. Ragtime thus began as a way of playing—a style of creative, syncopated transformation and embellishment of a melody. In the early days it was called "jig piano," referring back to the old minstrel dances, and favorite targets were old standards such as "Annie Laurie."

Capturing these folk ragtime ideas on paper was an art that evolved in the late '90's—most of the earliest scored syncopations were piano arrangements of popular songs done by schooled arrangers of the larger publishing houses.

The character of the rag was evolving: at first, a random collection of syncopated themes—medleys of idiomatic pop tunes such as the "coon songs," and occasionally genuine folk melodies—by 1897 the whole concept had matured; rags appeared which were organized collections of *original* syncopated themes. Ragtime was becoming a through-composed art, a piano literature. As the rag evolved, much form and flavor were derived from the march and the old-world dances. A rag is usually a construction of three to four separate strains; each one is played and then repeated (sometimes with embellishments), and the tune moves on to the next one. This concept is non-developmental in the classical sense, and unlike jazz, which evolves from improvisation on a theme. Within this discipline ragtime composers continued to find new ways to express themselves. The sound of a rag may vary from the formality of a Missouri classic to the bouncing rhythm of a fox-trot. It was a new music, a purely American concoction of formal and folk traditions. It expressed the imagination and dynamism of turn-of-the century America, when the country was young and adventuresome in spirit.

America was ready for the rag; the parlor piano was a fixture, a status symbol in American homes then, and more people made their own music, either by hand or by foot-pumping the pedals of the new pianola. Ragtime became our musical language for over two decades; it transformed our dancing, beginning with the cakewalk and evolving through the turkey trot of the 'teens.

But the rag did not arrive without a fight. A Coxey's Army of vociferous critics objected strenuously to the new ragged syncopations; taken as a group they were almost totally uninformed. In the early years they fussed and fumed that ragtime was the work of Satan —sinful and degenerate music of low-life origins. At least one tried to prove that merely hearing a rag could induce a spontaneous, involuntary reaction akin to an epileptic fit ("Ragtime: the New Tarantism"). Later on these bilious Brahmins confused the rags with the popular songs of the day and never mentioned Scott Joplin; it was a sign of what happened to the genuine article. Ragtime became a craze, a highly profitable business.

The popular song has always been the main staple

of the music business, and, as Tin Pan Alley moved closer to centralizing the entire publishing output of the country, America was flooded with syncopated songs and simple rags. At least by 1910 everything that was syncopated was called a rag. Much fine syncopated playing was widespread in arrangements and renditions of popular songs, especially on piano rolls—a continuation of the old tradition of creative performance and transformation. But the genuine rag was a separate, more complex instrumental conception, a more abstract form in the tradition of absolute music. The rags are the *crème de la crème*, one of our richest musical legacies.

The '70's have seen an unparalleled revival of ragtime, and a new academic interest in the form. America now thinks of ragtime more in terms of a graceful Scott Joplin rag than a fast, triple-forte rendition of an old pop song banged out on an out-of-tune upright piano. This is indeed a joyful progress for the genuine rag! Scott Joplin has at last intoxicated America with his beautiful, bittersweet classic rags.

The Missouri legacy of Scott Joplin and his peers is a rich one, to be sure, but not our total legacy of ragtime; it is high time to widen our scope, to appreciate all the other gifted men and women composers who syncopated with a flair. The present revival has centered on Joplin, barely allowing a glance at other composers. This single focus has thrown the rest of ragtime far *out* of focus. It has fostered a completely mistaken notion not only at the popular level, but also at the academic, that the classic Missouri school was the musical clearing house for all ragtime activity that preceded it, and the source, the inspiration for everything else that followed. The pioneer classic rag publisher, John Stark, helped perpetuate this myth in his hyperbolic ads which insisted that the Stark rags were the "simon pure," and that everything else was a "pale imitation." The label "classic rag" was an appropriate choice to proclaim the rags of Joplin, Scott, Lamb, et al., as truly immortal works. But the classic rag form was also just one way of organizing folk materials and writing ragtime. From 1897 on there were publishers all over the country who, like Stark, published ragtime they believed in. Composers and performers everywhere were producing excellent ragtime, and much of it was more syncopated, more "raggy" than the formal classic rag. The ragtime world outside the classic school was extremely variegated, and, outside of "Maple Leaf Rag," not everyone was familiar with the Stark catalogue. While Tin Pan Alley was opening new branches in the larger cities, small publishers, both rural and urban, were exercising the last vestige of pioneer initiative in publishing fine works of local talent.

The Missouri giants of course did have a great influence, especially on a second generation of ragtime composers who followed the classic rag tradition. But unless we are aware of the total spectrum of composing talent, of the variety of the ragtime expression, we have a one-dimensional view of ragtime. More important, we are missing a lot of good music. It is time to put the classic rag in proper perspective, to venture forth and embrace the rest of the ragtime world, to savor the charms of these rare ragtime jewels which have waited over a half-century to cast their syncopated spell.

Ragtime Rarities is a selection, an exploration of the actual majority output of rags which were being written all over America, from the early era of syncopated cakewalks on through the later fox-trot rags of the 'teens. The primary criterion used in selection was musical excellence within an overall intent to present as varied a collection as possible. Time-honored favorites too long unavailable, as well as generally unknown rags, were included to demonstrate the ebullient variety of expression in a form too often cited as stilted or stereotyped. While some of the compositions have the formality of the classic rag tradition, most are more direct, unpretentious expressions of an uncomplicated joyous spirit. Here is America at the turn of the century, syncopating from coast to coast.

N.B.: The pianist will please feel free to stomp the left foot.

II

The Stark Music Co., in addition to publishing the Missouri milestones, issued an interesting variety of other rags in the classic style, as well as more folksy conceptions. Whatever the tune, it was bound to fall heir to one of the legendary Stark blurbs: "The writer believes in very truth that Cole Smoak is a positive inspiration. Human language is not equal to the task of painting the interior thoughts of the soul. It is also certain that all souls do not slack their thirst from the same fountain. 'Cole Smoak' appeals to the writer in language unutterable. Would be pleased to hear from any who have heard the echo." "African Pas'" by St. Louis pianist Maurice Kirwin was one that Stark advertised as "easy and brilliant—good to catch the ragtime swing." He called attention to the fact that the "Climbers Rag" cover featured photos of the 1911 Cardinal baseball team, reproduced in halftone. Another St. Louis pianist and organist, Jerre Cammack, autographed and dated my copy of "Tom and Jerry Rag" in 1961. His note that it was written in 1906 reveals a frequent disparity between the time tunes were actually written and when they were finally published; Stark brought it out in 1917. "Cactus" and "Jinx" are two excellent rags by an overlooked St. Louis composer, Lucian Gibson. Both rags are stylistically close to Artie Matthews' "Pastimes" (reprinted in Dover's *Classic Piano Rags*). "Jinx," named after the famous cartoon character, was arranged by Matthews; Stark advertised it as "quaint and curious."

Much fine ragtime was issued by smaller St. Louis concerns. Placht & Son was a typical shoestring firm that published many fine folk rags; James Chapman and Leroy Smith's "One o' Them Things!" may in fact be the first instance of a scored twelve-bar blues pattern, a progenitor of a later blues/rag mix popular with most Black midwestern barrelhouse pianists. The Daniels, Russell & Boone company of St. Louis was apparently a short-lived enterprise that included Charles Daniels, who had already arranged Scott Joplin's first rag, and who later supervised much of the huge Remick company's publishing output. He and Russell finally headed west to San Francisco and published fine latter-day ragtime, including the wonderful "Whoa! Nellie!," once a favorite of the legendary West Coast pianist Paul Lingle. Frank Wooster was a local St. Louis composer who eventually sold his "Black Cat Rag" to John Stark. Popular St. Louis orchestra leader Dave Silverman (with Arthur Ward) wrote "That Hand Played Rag," a virtuoso piece that celebrates the advent of hand-played piano rolls and points the way to the novelty ragtime of the '20's.

In 1903 a ragtime talent that one day would rank second only to Scott Joplin was busy working for Dumars, a local music store in Carthage, Missouri. Young James Scott, though born in Neosho, Missouri, had been raised in Carthage, where his family had provided him with music lessons. His genius for ragtime composition blossomed in his first three tunes, all published by Dumars: "A Summer Breeze" and "The Fascinator" of 1903 and "On The Pike" of 1904. The latter celebrated the famous midway of the St. Louis World's Fair, where many of the nation's greatest ragtime pianists were playing that year.

Other outstate Missouri folk rags were "X. L. Rag" by legendary pianist L. Edgar Settle, published by the ancient A. W. Perry's Sons of Sedalia, and the two Blind Boone rag medleys. John W. Boone was a Black classical virtuoso who, much like his predecessor, Blind Tom Bethune. could play back any piece he heard, no matter how complex, after only one listening. In 1908 he retired from an incredible life of concert tours which had taken him all over the world. Black folk music had always been a part of his repertoire, and, upon retiring to his Columbia, Missouri, home, he had two medleys published which preserved favorite local Negro melodies.

The House of Lords was a prominent sporting house in the active mining town of Joplin, in the southwest corner of Missouri. The first-floor saloon featured ragtime, and many of the great pioneers played there, including Scott Joplin. A Black gambler, Babe La Tour, used to sneak in a wide-eyed local boy named Percy Wenrich, who hid behind the piano and soaked up the pure syncopated folk strains. This early experience, combined with a natural flair for melodiousness, eventually made Wenrich one of the most prolific and successful composers of his day. He left for Chicago when only a teenager, and later lived in New York, but he returned regularly to Joplin for inspiration. Though he is best remembered for his fine songs like "Put On Your Old Gray Bonnet" and "When You Wore a Tulip," he wrote and performed fine rags, including "Peaches and Cream" and "Dixie Blossoms."

In the nearby town of Braymer, an aspiring brain surgeon, C. L. Woolsey, was working his way through medical school writing rags. "Mashed Potatoes" and the extraordinary "Medic Rag" are two of the finest idiomatic midwestern rags ever done.

Kansas City, Missouri, was an important ragtime center from the early days. The Carl Hoffman publishing house, which had brought out Joplin's "Original Rags" in 1899, issued in 1901 the folksy "Peaceful Henry" by E. Harry Kelly, a vaudevillian who once had a dog act. The title was inspired by the congenial janitor of the publishing house. Another local character, a champion cakewalker, was immortalized in " 'Doc' Brown's Cake Walk" by Charles L. Johnson, best remembered for his "Dill Pickles" of 1906. Johnson's first tunes were written for his mandolin band in the '90's, and " 'Doc' Brown" was his first rag. The comments below the photo of "Doc" Brown indicate that the tune is intended to be more complex than the traditional cakewalk conception. Most ragtime publishing in Kansas City later was centered in the J.W. Jenkins' Sons Music Co., whose "Cotton Patch" was one of their many fine local rags.

Some of the earliest syncopated sounds were probably heard in Chicago in 1893. The Columbian Exposition that year attracted vital talent in ragtime's formative years: Ben Harney, W. C. Handy, Will Marion Cook and Scott Joplin, who performed there with his own band. Some of the earliest rags came out of Chicago in 1897, including the first copyrighted rag, "Mississippi Rag" by William H. Krell. A year later the publisher Brainard issued an even more intriguing tune by this Chicago bandleader, "Shake Yo' Dusters!" The pioneering Thompson Music Co. published a jewel of early ragtime in "Louisiana Rag" by Theodore Northrup, an early figure who codified syncopation that same year for the *Ben Harney Rag-*

time Instructor. The Victor Kremer Co. of Chicago published much music in commemoration of the World's Fair of 1904 in St. Louis. The "St. Louis Tickle" was a hit at the fair and became one of the most beloved rags of all time. Its second strain was a notorious bit of musical low-life. It is generally credited to legendary New Orleans cornetist Buddy Bolden, but it pops up in several early rags, and was well known in Missouri. Though the tune is credited to the mysterious duo "Barney & Seymore," it may actually have been written by Pierce City, Missouri, composer Theron C. Bennett. The energetic Bennett went to work for Kremer that year, and later became a publisher himself. He went west finally to operate the famous Dutch Mill in Denver (see the store stamp on the cover of "Encore Rag"). He is the actual composer of the ambitious "Sweet Pickles," and other editions give him due credit (using aliases was great sport among many ragtime composers).

The Pioneer Music Publishing Company issued the idiomatic "Glad Cat Rag," with its funky chromaticism and phrasing typical of midwestern piano playing. Another large Chicago publisher who began printing rags in 1897 was Will Rossiter. "The Stinging Bee" was one of several fine tunes of Mike Bernard, who studied Ben Harney and became the most popular ragtime pianist of his day. At the turn of the century there was very little piano recording, but he did solos for Columbia and, with his flashy technique, was an inevitable winner of piano contests in the early era.

When W. C. Handy's "Memphis Blues" of 1912 first became popular, it ushered in a new "blues" craze. In those days before the invention of the word jazz, genuine blues, including the "St. Louis Blues," were published as *ragtime* tunes, or "Blue Rags." And a feeling for the blues, which seems to have always been integral to the Black midwestern piano style, began to tinge the traditional ragtime tunes. "The Original Chicago Blues" is an ineresting amalgam of both rag and blues ideas.

The extraordinary ragtime at Nashville could well be called a *school* of folk rag composition. There is a consistent style here—an inspired spontaneity and an unfettered approach characteristic of good folk rag, and an ebullient mix of both Black folk sources and White Tennessee hill music, a distinctly "southern-fried" concoction. The leading composer was blind pianist Charles Hunter, who worked for the Jesse French Piano Co. in Nashville until 1902, when he was transferred to the St. Louis branch. The charms of the urban wine-room sporting life were a Venus's-flytrap for the Tennessee country boy; he died around 1907 of tuberculosis. His excellent "Just Ask Me" was issued by Frank Fite; Fite and H. A. French were the

two leading publishers of Nashville ragtime. The first Nashville rag to appear, however, was by one Thomas Broady in 1898, "Mandy's Broadway Stroll." This and his "Whittling Remus" are fetching combinations of cakewalk and country rag, while his "Tennessee Jubilee" is an open-ended essay, with each strain in a new key.

A publisher who specialized in music of the lower Mississippi Valley was O. K. Houck, with branches in Little Rock, Memphis and New Orleans. "Encore Rag" has at least one floating folk strain: its second strain is identical to one in a classic barrelhouse recording by Will Ezell, "Bucket of Blood."

The ragtime of New Orleans is another study in a regional style. While the sporting district of Storyville boasted some of the nation's greatest "professors," as per Jelly Roll Morton, the published rags are very rough-hewn in comparison with the contemporary output in St. Louis.

"Sponge," published very near Storyville, is a singular piece of ragtime, a haunting comment on the underground ("sponge" in local slang probably referred to pimping, or at least cadging). Alternating between major and minor chords, it weaves a poignant ambivalent mood—an aura of pungent charms and dark resignation, a true glimpse of the "sporting life."

The Ohio Valley became a hotbed of ragtime and the center of a second generation of gifted midwestern composers. Cincinnati had a long heritage of Black music which centered in the riverfront area, as was the case with most river towns. It was here that Stephen Foster picked up ideas from musical Black watermen in the 1840's. "The Rag Pickers Rag" is an exposition of syncopation, one of several excellent Robert J. O'Brien rags. During the ragtime era, most recreation on the river at Cincinnati centered on the steamer *Island Queen*, celebrated in Willis' "Queen Rag" and in "Chimes" by local calliope player and excellent ragtime composer Homer Denney. The local publishing house John Arnold & Co. was probably very small, but its limited output was extremely ambitious, including at least three topnotch rags, one of which was "The Sheath."

Two rags that sparked much of the Ohio Valley creativity were May Aufderheide's "Dusty Rag" and "Thriller Rag," of 1908 and '09, respectively. They were published by May's father, an Indianapolis stockbroker, and became nationwide hits. The legendary New Orleans cornetist Bunk Johnson recalled them both and recorded them years later. "That Demon Rag," sporting an arresting Dantesque monster on the cover, is a brilliant Indianapolis rag by Black composer Russell Smith. But the most incredible work to come out of the area is probably "The Lion Tamer Rag" of New Albany, Indiana. Mark Janza's piece is truly a "fantasia," with surprising harmonies and syncopations, a labyrinth of inspired ragtime.

Indeed, some of the most inspired and inventive ragtime came from small-town composers. The familiar saga of "Car-Barlick-Acid," in fact, reveals how larger eastern publishers were gaining eventual control of the music business. The composer, Clarence Wiley, was an aspiring pharmacist who published the tune himself in his home town of Oskaloosa, Iowa, in 1903. Almost immediately this fine rag was bought by the Giles Bros. of the river towns of Quincy, Illinois, and Hannibal, Missouri; in fact, their store stamp is on this first-edition copy here. As the tune became more and more popular, Witmark of New York snapped it up.

In Moline, Illinois, a most amazing composition appeared, named "Jungle Time," subtitled rightfully "A Genuine Rag." It is a bold, folk-inspired conception, highlighted by a twenty-bar strain, an idea Scott Joplin used later. Composer E. P. Severin was a local trombonist.

In Detroit, Theodore Finney's orchestra had established a dynasty of Black musicians in the late nineteenth century, and they controlled the union as well, an unheard of situation at the time. Fred S. Stone took over the orchestra after Finney's death. "Ma Rag Time Baby" was his best excursion into ragtime. His colleague, Harry P. Guy, is credited with the first ragtime waltz, "Echoes from the Snowball Club" of 1898. The cover of his excellent " 'Cleanin' Up' in Georgia" makes use of the famous American Tobacco Co. cakewalk ads; a more primitive drawing of one of these was used on the original Sedalia, Missouri, edition of "Maple Leaf Rag."

An undeniable Texas blues influence sparks "Majestic Rag," a down-home barrelhouse rag with walking bass, breaks and phrasing indigenous to the piano playing of the Southwest.

"Felix Rag" by H. H. McSkimming of Kiowa, Kansas, is indeed "phenomenal" in its use of extended 3 over 4 syncopations and its overall conception. Such an eccentric, creative small-town rag defies the simpler, more formulated rags of Tin Pan Alley being cranked out in the urban centers.

The ragtime scene in New York City was characterized by a dichotomy that reflected, in larger dimensions, the situation in most other urban centers. On the one hand was a vast competitive network of commercial publishing, the home of Tin Pan Alley; on the other was a vast underground of the black idiomatic ragtime of the Harlem keyboard giants, such as Eubie Blake and James P. Johnson. The Harlem rags

were too complex to interest the publishers, and it was not until 1913 that a Harlem classic (Luckey Roberts' "Pork and Beans") was published, and then only after it was simplified and packaged according to the current trends. The big publishers were more interested in selling a hit song or a rag that almost anyone could play on the parlor piano; thus many of the earliest New York rag publications derived from the coon-song craze of the 1890's. Max Hoffman's "Ragtown Rags" is actually a medley of coon-song hits arranged for piano. Several such early publications are paced much like a small revue, and reflect the tremendous influence of the theater on New York music.

The cakewalk grew from plantation folk roots into a professional and social dance of astounding proportions, sparking a nearly world-wide cakewalk craze during the late 90's. It was the beginning of a truly idiomatic popular American dance tradition. The demand for cakewalk dance music soon brought about the cakewalk as a compositional form, which set the stage for the rags. Cakewalks were basically marches spiced with syncopation, and quickly became one of the hottest Tin Pan Alley commodities. Hundreds of them were written and published in New York, bearing such distant, romantic references as "Alabama Dream," "Georgia Sunset" and "Mobile Prance." The best cakewalk writers had a flair for a kind of idiomatic melodiousness. One of the most successful was Frederick Allen "Kerry" Mills, whose "At a Georgia Campmeeting" of 1897 has become permanently identified with the dance. "Impecunious Davis," with typical notes on its origins, was one of Mills' best. The first cakewalk hit, however, was "Eli Green's Cake Walk," written by song-plugger Sadie Koninsky in 1896. In 1898 Stern issued the instrumental arrangement with an additional strain, included here. The cover of "Alabama Dream" presents the dress for the formal cakewalk dance. The splendiferous lady's gown and the gentleman's top hat and cane were traditional apparel. "Coon Hollow Capers" was part of the repertoire of the Queen City Concert Band of Sedalia, Missouri, in which Scott Joplin once played second cornet. "Bunch o' Blackberries" is one of several cakewalk hits of Abe Holzmann, whose "Flying Arrow" in this collection documents the "Indian intermezzo," a subcraze of the ragtime era which romanticized the American Indian. "Sure Fire," another Indian cover, is by the mystery man of ragtime, Henry E. Lodge. Almost nothing is known of Lodge, one of the most talented and prodigious composers in the idiom. Cakewalk composer Joseph Gearen added a rare fillip to his "Big Foot Lou" of 1899. He suggested "Rag Time" variations on the regular melody in the finale. This touch brings more syncopation to the simple cakewalk format, and provides for a creative, rousing finish, a performance tradition that lives on in jazz.

The excellent "Watermelon Trust" is a good example of serious ragtime composition, one of many that came out of New York.

By the 'teens, the bouncy fox-trot and the faster one-step had taken over from the cakewalk and the slow-drag two-step. Animal dances were the rage: "The Bunny Hug," "Lobster Glide," "Baboon Bounce," "Kangaroo Hop," "The Turkey Trot." Most of the rags written during this time made more adventurous use of harmony, and there was more jazz coloration in the phrasing. Harry Jentes' "Bantam Step" is a haunting, very original contribution to the dance menagerie. The art form was evolving, becoming more complex and demanding. After 1920 ragtime became "novelty piano," more the domain of professional pianists than an idiom for the home market.

TREBOR JAY TICHENOR

St. Louis, Mo.
Autumn, 1974

CONTENTS

Publisher, city and date are in parentheses.

page

DUSTY

· RAG ·

By May Aufderheide.

Published by
J. H. Aufderheide.
Lemcke, Bldg.
INDIANAPOLIS.

104

5

DUSTY.

MAY AUFDERHEIDE.

THE THRILLER

RAG

By
MAY
Aufderheide
COMPOSER OF
"BUZZER RAG"
"DUSTY" &
"RICHMOND RAG."

CENTRAL
CLEV'D

"Ragtime Bob" DARCH
P.O. BOX 323, VIRGINIA CITY, NEV.

5

J.H.AUFDERHEIDE
MUSIC PUBLISHER LEMCKE
BUILDING
INDIANAPOLIS, IND.

The Thriller!
RAG.

MAY AUFDERHEIDE.
Composer of "Buzzer Rag,"
"Dusty" and "Richmond Rag."

Not fast.

May Aufderheide

ALABAMA DREAM

(Rag-Time Cake Walk)

BY

GEO. D. BARNARD.

Piano Solo	50.	2 Mandolins & Guitar.	50.
Mandolin Solo	30.	Mandolin & Piano	50.
2 Mandolins	40.	2 Mandolins & Piano	60.
Mandolin & Guitar	40.	2 Mandolins, Piano & Guitar.	70.

PUBLISHED ALSO FOR BAND & ORCHESTRA.

THE JOHN CHURCH COMPANY.

CINCINNATI.   NEW YORK.   CHICAGO.

LEIPSIC.   LONDON.

Alabama Dream.

A RAG TIME CAKE WALK.

Published also for Band and Orchestra.

GEORGE D. BARNARD.

Tempo di Marcia.

TRIO.

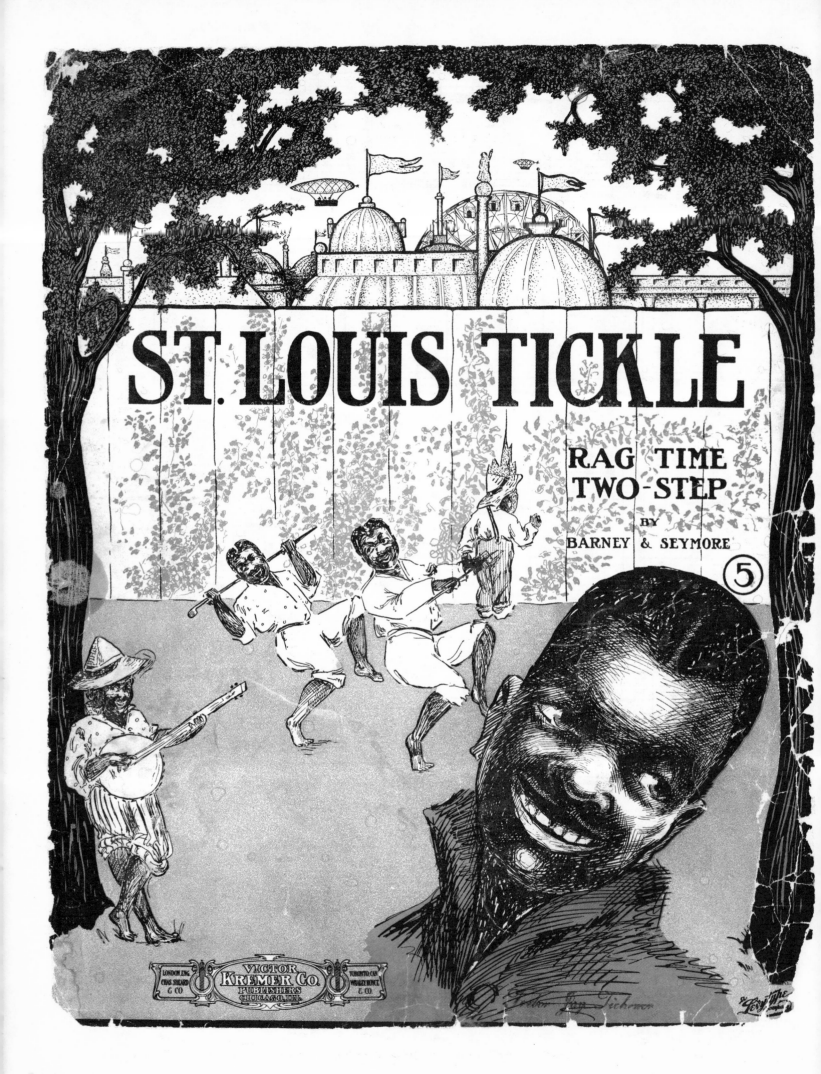

ST. LOUIS TICKLE

Tempo Niggerino

BARNEY & SEYMORE

16 · *"Barney & Seymore"* (Theron C. Bennett?)

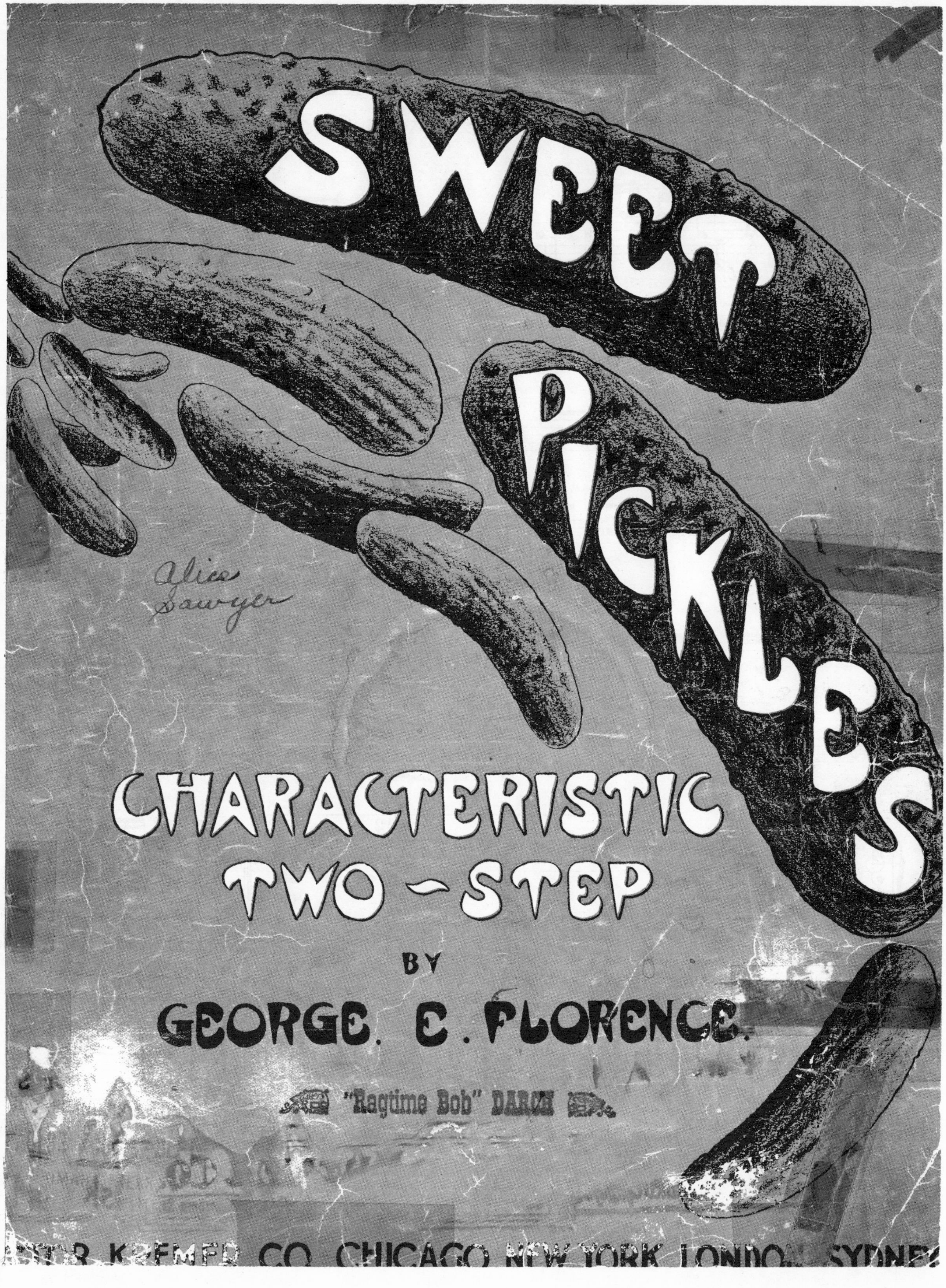

SWEET PICKLES

Alice Sawyer

CHARACTERISTIC TWO - STEP

BY

GEORGE. E. FLORENCE.

"Ragtime Bob" DARCH

...TER KREMER CO CHICAGO NEW YORK LONDON SYDNEY

SWEET PICKLES
Characteristic Two-Step

By GEO. E. FLORENCE

A-REAL-RAG-TIME-TWO-STEP

THE STINGING BEE

Characteristic

BY THE
FAMOUS PIANIST

MIKE BERNARD

THE PUBLIC'S FAVORITE

Published for
BAND & ORCHESTRA

WILL ROSSITER
MUSIC PUBLISHER
CHICAGO ILL.
Albert & Son, Sydney Australia
Copyright MCMXVI by Will Rossiter

5

THE STINGING BEE
Characteristic.

BY
MIKE BERNARD.
The World's greatest Rag-time Player.

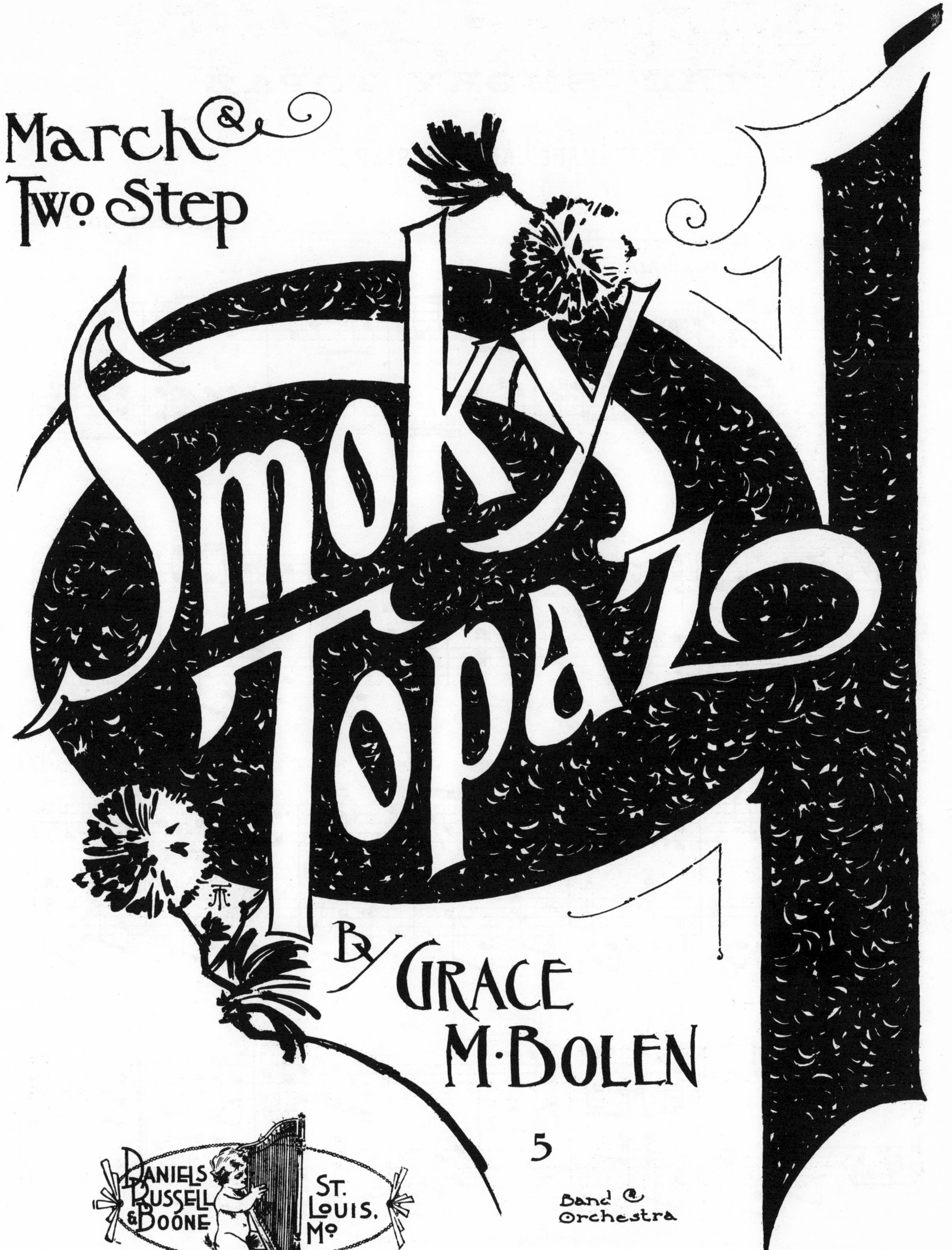

March & Two Step

Smoky Topaz

By Grace M. Bolen

Daniels Russell & Boone
St. Louis, Mo.

5

Band & Orchestra

"THE SMOKY TOPAZ"

MARCH AND TWO STEP.

GRACE M. BOLEN.

Tempo di Cakewalk.

BLIND BOONE'S

SOUTHERN
RAG MEDLEY

№ ONE
Strains From The Alleys.

Published by
ALLEN MUSIC CO.
908 Broadway
COLUMBIA. MO.

Boone's Rag Medley Nº 1.

I got a chick - en on my back   There's a

bull   dog   on   my track   But I'll   make   it   to   my

shack   'Fore   day.   Oh

Make me a pall   et   on   a   your   floor

Oh, no Babe!

I'm a goin' to tell you the truth I cer-tain-ly does love dat yel-low man I'm a goin to buy him all the cig-ar-ettes and chew-ing gum a thet I can I'm a goin

Otto Zimmerman & Son.
Music Printer & Eng.
Cincinnati Ohio.

BLIND BOONE'S

SOUTHERN

RAG MEDLEY

Nº TWO

STRAINS FROM THE FLAT BRANCH.

Published by

ALLEN MUSIC CO.

908 Broadway
COLUMBIA, MO.

RAG MEDLEY NO II.

Strains from Flat Branch.

BLIND BOONE.

Carrie's gone to Kan-sas City She's done gone and I'm go - ing too

So they say.

Oh! hon – ey   ain't you   sor – ry

CODA.

MANDY'S BROADWAY STROLL

A GENUINE RAG-TIME MARCH.

BY THOS. E. BROADY.

5º

Published by H. A. FRENCH. NASHVILLE, TENN.

Mandy's Broadway Stroll.

Arr. by EUGENE V. NELSON.

THOS. E. BROADY.

Tempo di Rag.

TRIO.

A TENNESSEE JUBILEE.
RAG-TIME MARCH AND TWO STEP.
Published by
H.A. FRENCH
Nashville, Tenn.
BY THOS. E. BROADY.
Composer of Mandys Broadway Stroll.
5

A TENNESSEE JUBILEE.

THOS. E. BROADY.

Composer of
Mandy's Broadway Stroll

WHITTLING REMUS.

A RAGTIME MARCH.

5

PUBLISHED BY
H. A. FRENCH.
NASHVILLE, TENN.

BY
THOS. E. BROADY
COMPOSER OF
"A TENNESSEE JUBILEE"
AND
"MANDY'S BROADWAY STROLL"
TWO OF THE LATEST RAGTIME FAVORITES.

BRANDON PRINTING CO., NASHVILLE.

WHITTLING REMUS

THOS. E. BROADY.

Composer of "A Tennessee Jubilee"
and "Mandys Broadway Stroll."

Trio.

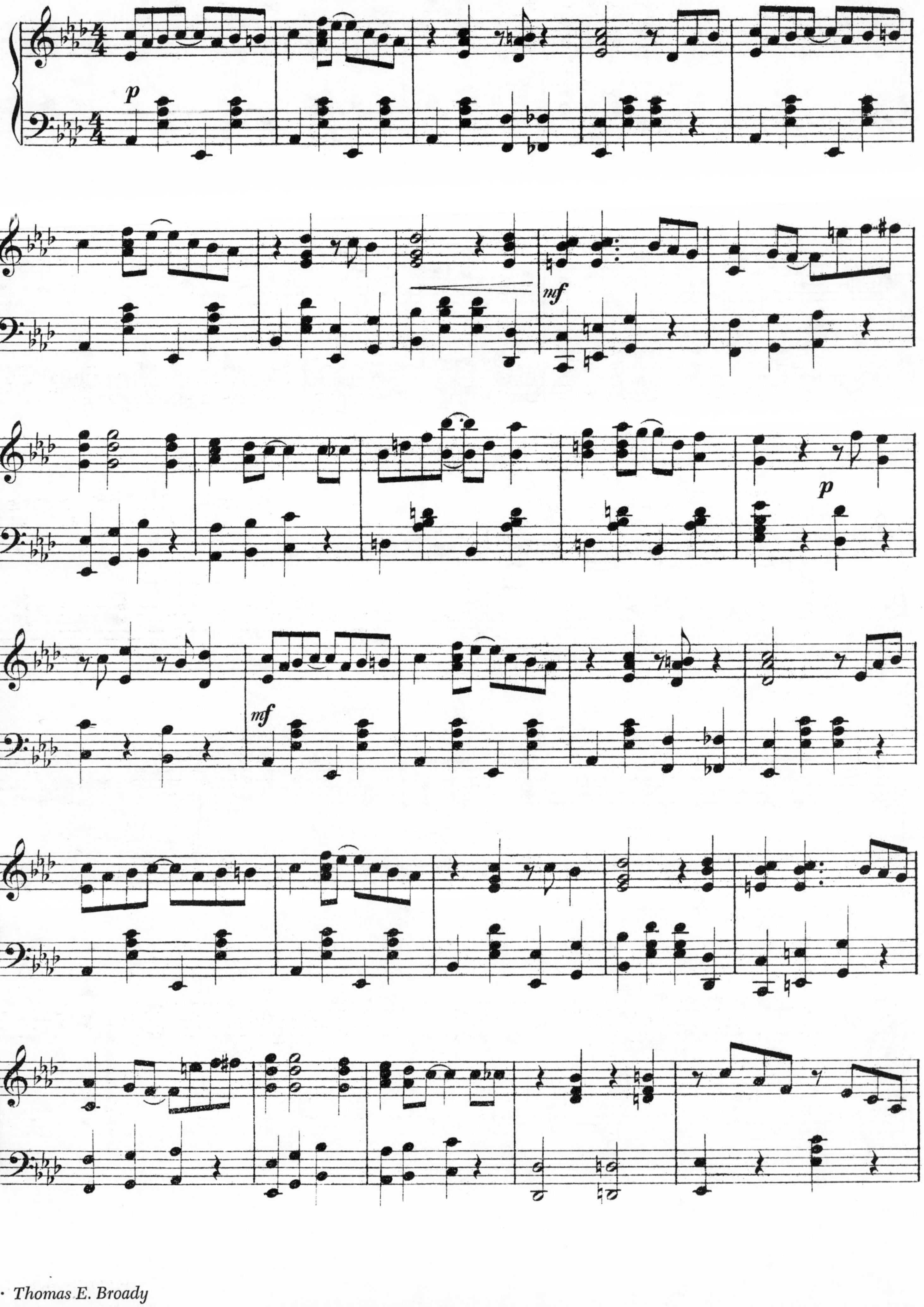

To Tom Pickeral Some Drummer

Tom and Jerry

RAG

JERRY CAMMACK

Slowly

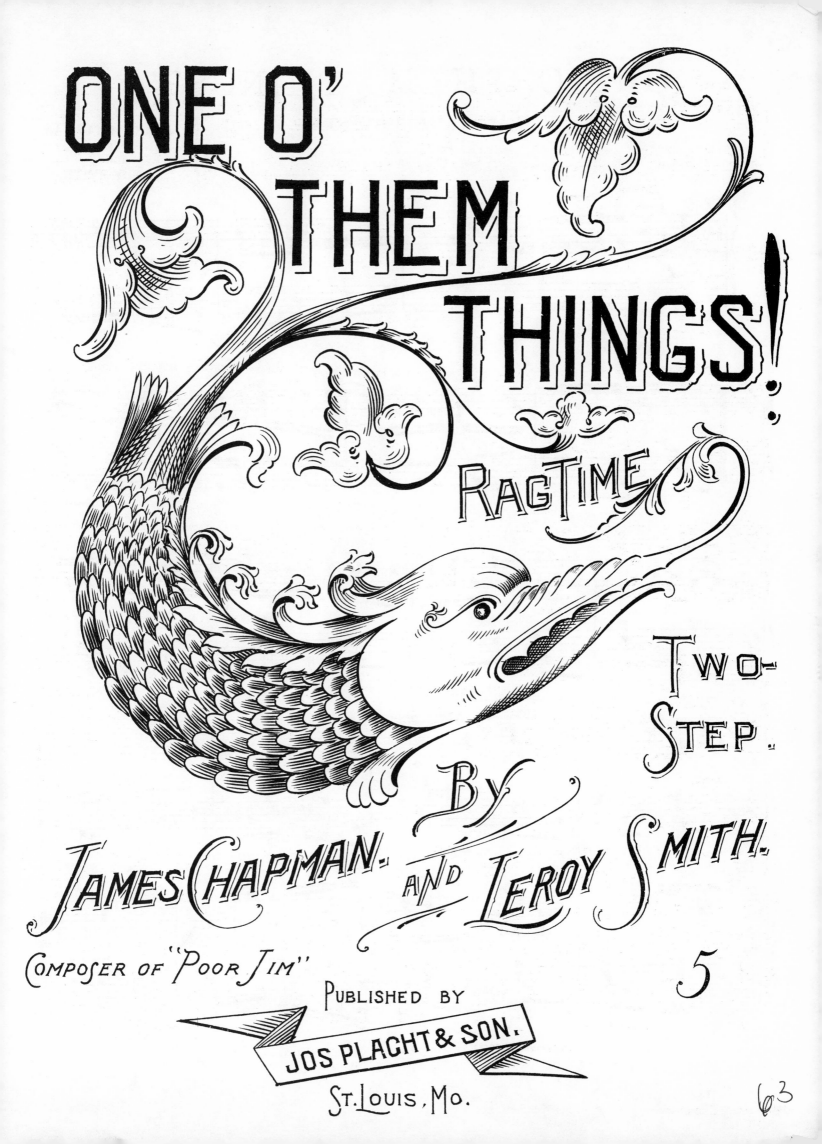

ONE O, THEM THINGS?

RAG TIME TWO-STEP.

By { JAMES CHAPMAN Composer of "POOR JIM" and LEROY SMITH.

CHIMES

Mrs. Lelah M. Curtis

A NOVELTY RAG

HOMER DENNEY

By

AS
PLAYED NIGHTLY
ON
STEAMER
ISLAND
QUEEN

H. R. McCLURE
SIDNEY,
OHIO.
PUBLISHERS
COMPANY,
OHIO.

Composer of
"HOT CABBAGE"
"CHEESE &
CRACKERS"
"TANGLE FINGERS
RAG"

CHIMES
A Novelty Rag.

HOMER DENNEY

TRIO

ENCORE RAG

TAD FISCHER

Intro.

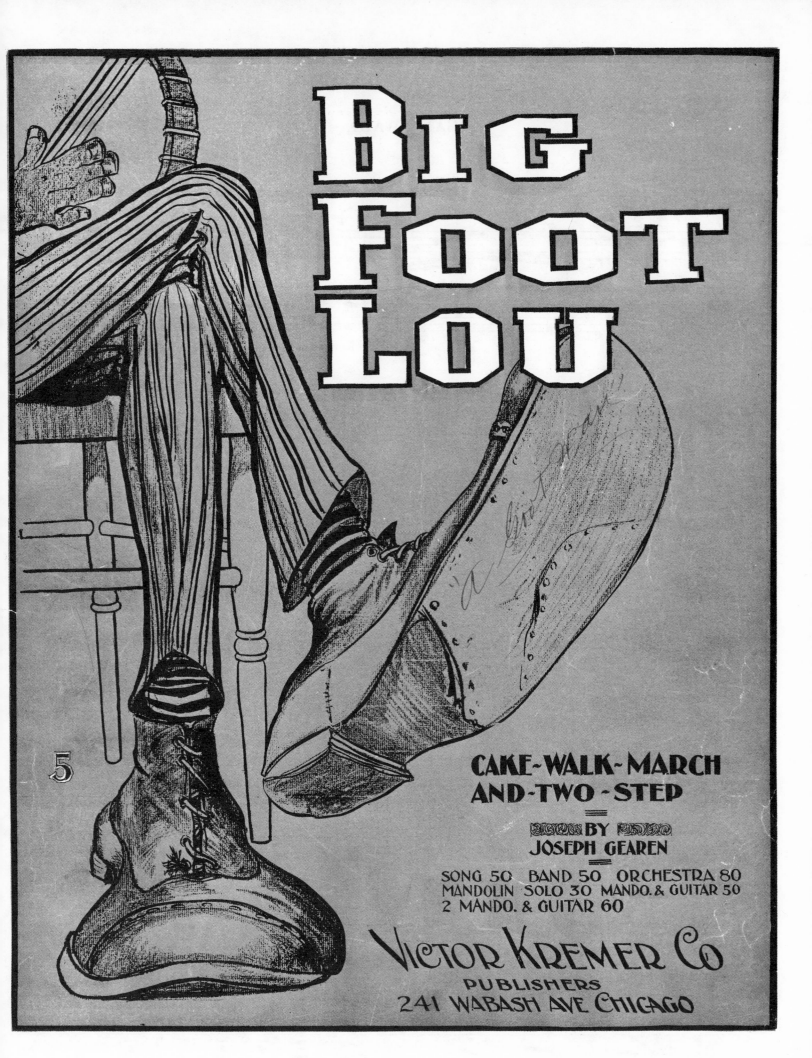

BIG FOOT LOU.

CAKE WALK.

PIANO SOLO.

Jos. Gearen.

JINX RAG

Dedicated to the famous cartoonist Jean Knott

LUCIAN P. GIBSON

PUBLISHERS OF RagTime THAT IS DIFFERENT
STARK MUSIC CO.
ST. LOUIS. MO.
127 EAST 23 ST.
NEW YORK.

JINX RAG.

Not fast - Don't fake.

By LUCIAN P. GIBSON.
Arr. by Artie Matthews.

Soft and dream-like.

TRIO.

Brilliante.

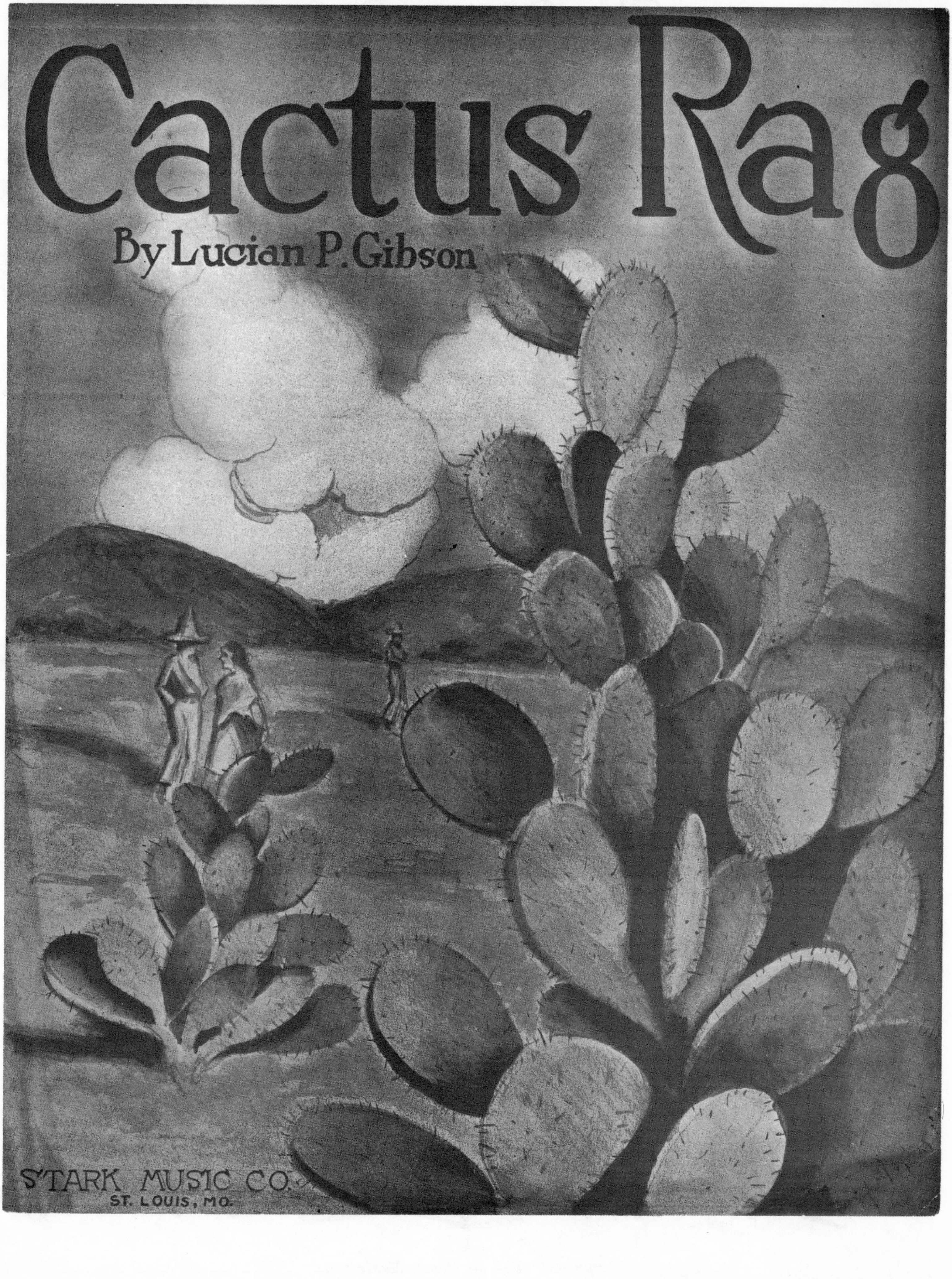

Cactus Rag
By Lucian P. Gibson
STARK MUSIC CO.
ST. LOUIS, MO.

The Cactus Rag

LUCIAN PORTER GIBSON
Composer of Jinx Rag.

Moderato

TRIO

Coon Hollow Capers

MARCH AND TWO-STEP

By

FRANK R. GILLIS.

WORDS BY
W. MURDOCH LIND.
WHICH MAY BE SUNG AD LIBITUM.

NEW YORK.

PUBLISHED BY **CONNOR & GILLIS.** 6 EAST. 14TH ST.

COPYRIGHT 1899 BY CONNOR & GILLIS.

"Coon Hollow Capers."
March and Two Step.

Words by W. MURDOCH LIND.

Music by FRANK R. GILLIS.

Which may be sung ad lib.

Copyright 1899, by Connor & Gillis.

Trio.

We'se g'wine to have a spree,
out for a good old time,

Come jine de jam-bo - ree; Swell coons of high de - gree. Won't miss dis grand oc-ca-sion.
Tick-ets are but a dime; La-dies neat and sub-lime, Of black-an' tan per-suasion,

Check ra - zors at de door, Don't bring dem on de floor, If you get gay you'll be ar-
All hope to win dat cake, Don't make no fun-ny break, Walk on, you nig-gers, till de

1.
res - ted, sho's you born! For we are
2.
break-in' of de morn. Just see de gals in de gal -'ry, Oh me, Oh

my! Sweet-er than pie, Dat ain't no lie! An' dar's de cake up a-

yon-der smi-ling an' white, Coon Hol-low ca-pers will be cut here to - night.

Whoa! Nellie!

(STOP RAG.)

By GEORGE GOULD.

Moderato.

✻Stopping here, leaves dancers without music — very effective. "Whoa! Nellie!" to be shouted.

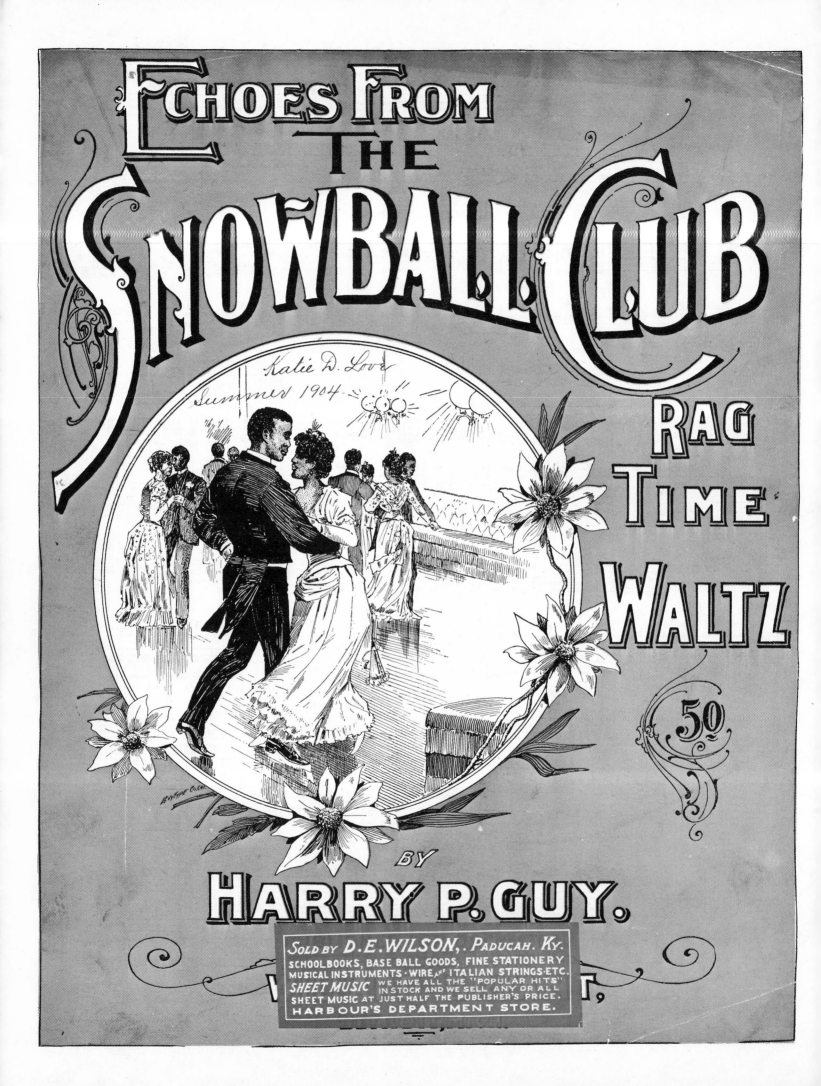

ECHOES FROM THE SNOWBALL CLUB.

ORIGINAL RAG TIME WALTZ.

HARRY P. GUY.

Dan Bryant, Music Typographer, Detroit, Mich.

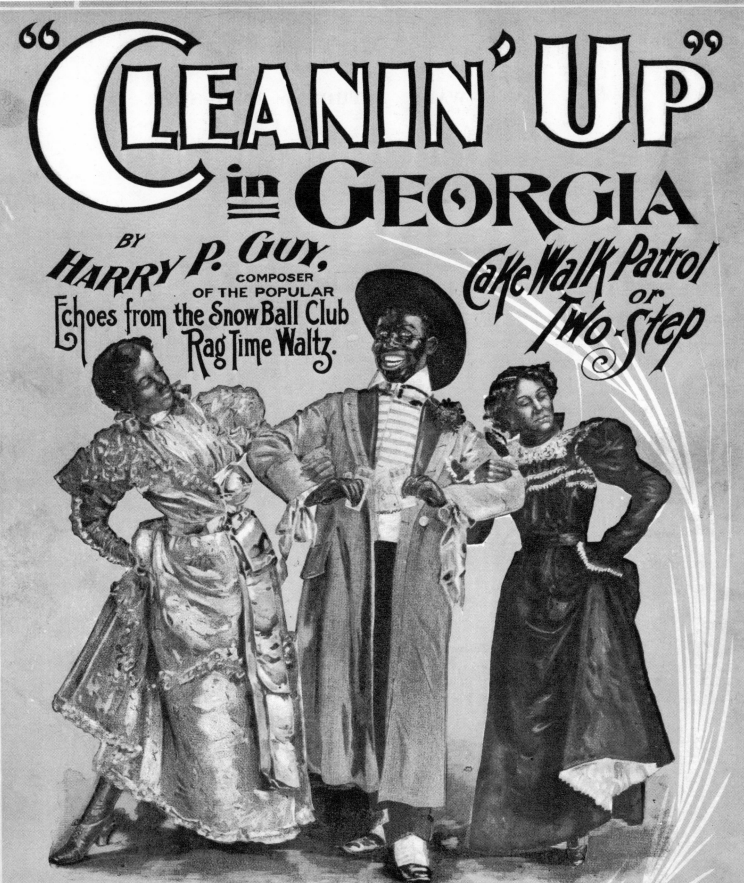

"Cleanin' Up" in Georgia

BY HARRY P. GUY, COMPOSER OF THE POPULAR Echoes from the Snow Ball Club Rag Time Waltz.

Cake Walk Patrol or Two-Step

Old Virginia Adv.-By Permission of Amer. Tobacco Co.

Published Complete in all Arrangements WILLARD BRYANT, DETROIT, MICH.

 50

"CLEANIN' UP" IN GEORGIA.

CAKE-WALK PATROL or TWO-STEP.

HARRY P. GUY.

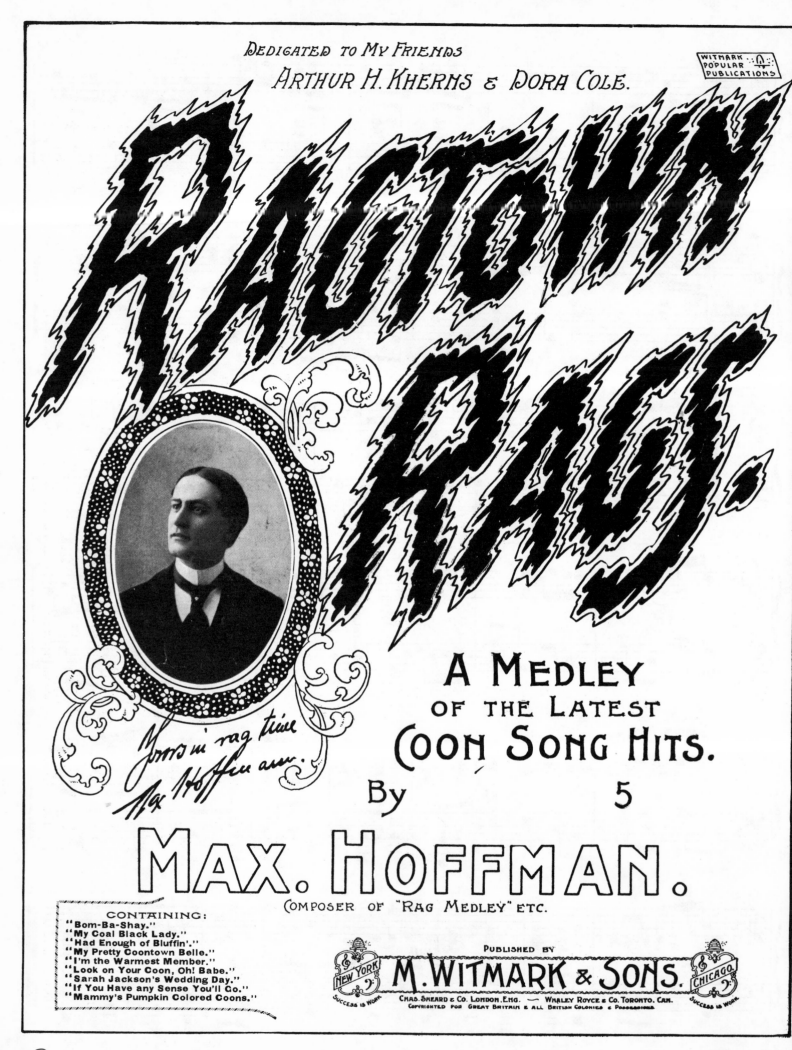

"RAGTOWN RAGS."

By MAX HOFFMAN.

"Look on your coon oh Babe." *ANDERSON*.

"Bom-Ba-Shay." *HOFFMANN*.

"Mammy's Little Pumpkins Colored

Coons." *(HILLMAN & PERRIN.)*

"If you've got any sense you'll go." (HARNEY.)

"My Pretty Coontown Belle" (HILLMAN & PERRIN.)

Coal Black Lady.

"I'm the warm-

est member in the land." GEARY.

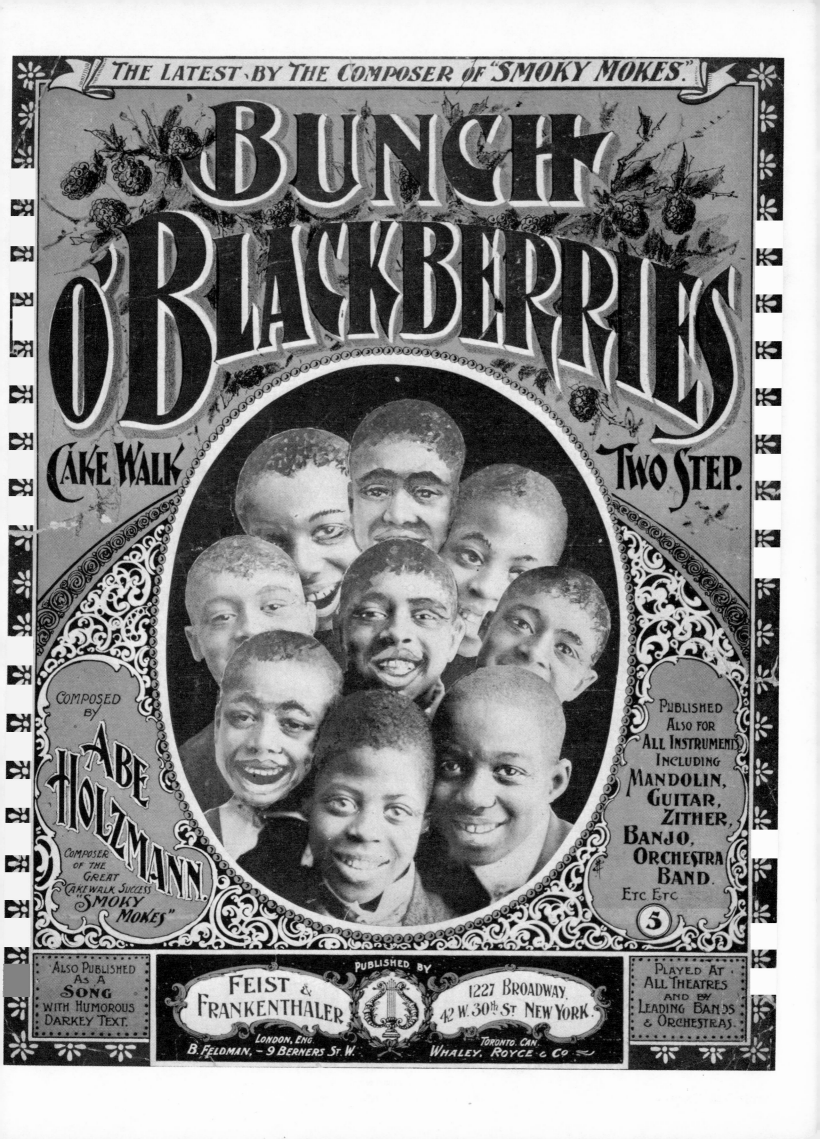

BUNCH O' BLACKBERRIES.

Cake-Walk & Two-Step.

by Abe Holzmann.
Composer of Smoky Mokes.
Cake Walk & Two-Step.

Flying Arrow.

Intermezzo Indienne.

March & Two Step.

By ABE HOLZMANN.

Composer of { BLAZE AWAY & UNCLE SAMMY MARCHES
SYMPHIA & LOVELAND WALTZES.

Trio.

March D.C.

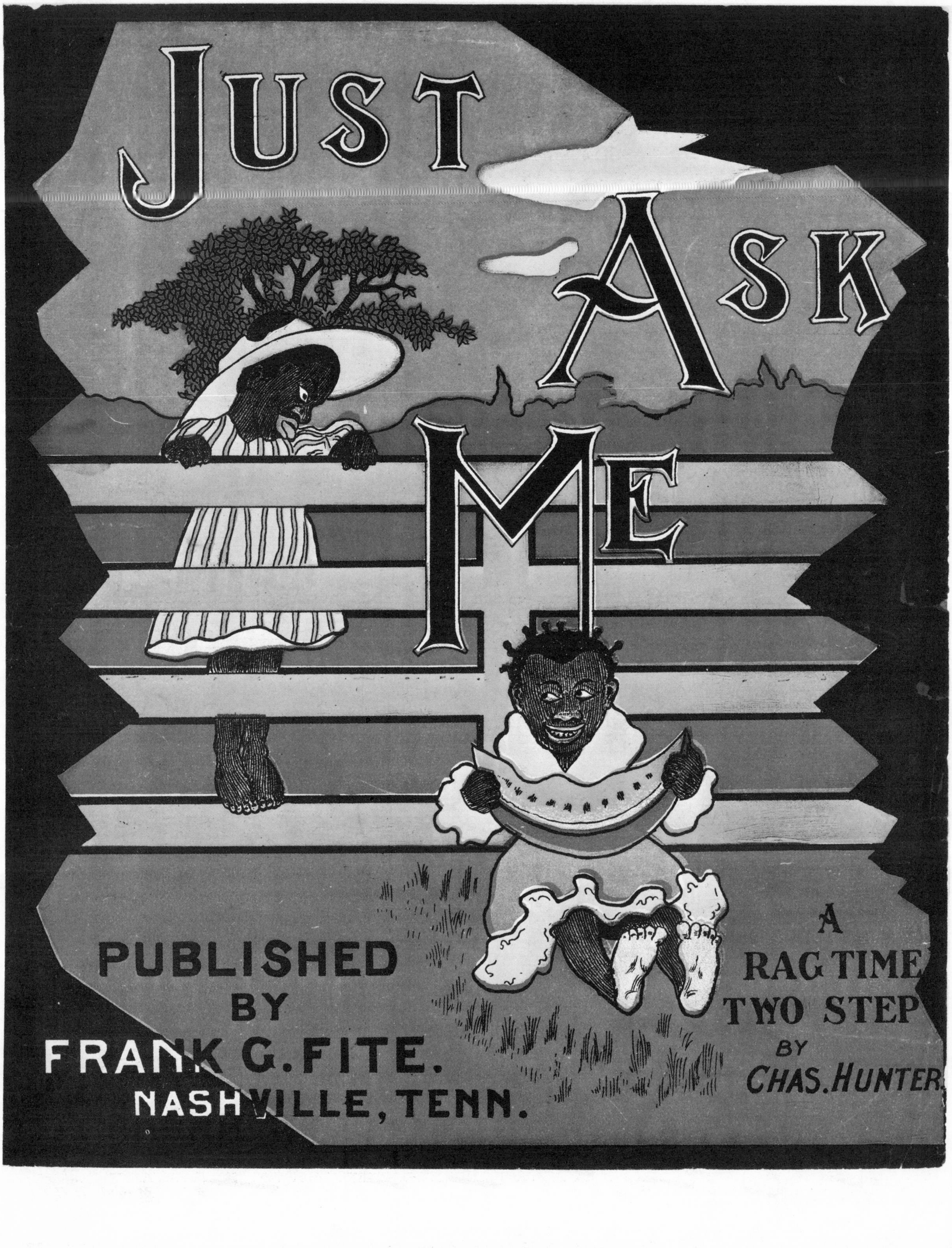
JUST ASK ME
PUBLISHED
BY
FRANK G. FITE.
NASHVILLE, TENN.
A
RAG TIME
TWO STEP
BY
CHAS. HUNTER.

JUST ASK ME.

Ragtime March and Two Step.

CHAS HUNTER.

Moderato.

127

Otto Zimmerman
Music Printer
Cincinnati, O.

LION TAMER

A · SYNCOPATED · FANTASIA ·

by Mark Janza..

⑤

"Ragtime Bob" DARCH

A.F.MARZIAN
MUSIC PUBLISHER
NEW ALBANY,
IND.

Foster's Music House
Rockland, Me.

DEAN
CORNWELL

The Lion Tamer Rag
A SYNCOPATED FANTASIA

MARK JANZA

Moderato

TRIO

BANTAM STEP
INSTRUMENTAL
BY
HARRY JENTES
L. M. Goodyear
Trebor Jay Tichenor
Published by
Shapiro, Bernstein & Co.
MUSIC
PUBLISHERS
224 West 47TH Street
New York

Bantam Step

FOX TROT M.M. ♩= 88
ONE-STEP M.M. ♩= 126

By HARRY JENTES

PIANO

TRIO

THE
ORIGINAL
KANSAS CITY RAG.

DOC- BROWN'S

CAKE WALK.

KANSAS
CITY

COMPOSED BY
CHAS. L. JOHNSON.

K.C. ENG. CO.

PUBLISHED BY
J.W.
JENKINS'
SONS
MUSIC
CO.

Piano Solo,	$ .50
Mandolin and Guitar,	.40
2 Mandolins and Guitar,	.50
3 Mandolins and Guitar,	.60
1 Mandolin and Piano,	.50
2 Mandolins and Piano,	.60
3 Mandolins and Piano,	.70
Mandolin Orchestra,	1.00
Banjo Solo,	.30
Banjo Duet,	.40
Orchestra, full,	.75
Orchestra, 14 parts,	.60
Orchestra, 10 parts,	.50
Orchestra, Piano Accompaniment, extra,	.15
Military Band,	1.00

"DOC" BROWN.

There is probably no city or town in the country that does not contain a peculiar character—one who is singled out on account of doing certain things that no one else would think of doing, or using strange language that seems senseless, but nevertheless has a meaning which is readily understood when the listener can see the speaker, or other eccentric traits which make these characters a special object for comment.

Of all such that may exist there is probably not one of them that compares with the subject of this sketch for original mirth-provoking characteristics.

"Doc" Brown is noted in Kansas City and vicinity for the many comical and unusual things he does and says but as the "Champion Cake Walker" of the country is where he shines. He has met all comers in this line and has never failed to "take the cake" with one exception, namely, in St. Louis several years ago. The judges at this contest were conceded to be unfair by everyone present. hence this is not considered a defeat.

The rythm commonly called the "Cake Walk" is departed from in this composition purposely with the hope that this style may find as hearty approval as the old.

THE AUTHOR.

"DOC." BROWN'S CAKE WALK.

KANSAS CITY RAG.

CHAS L. JOHNSON.

TRIO.

Dedicated to CHAS. L. JOHNSON.

PEACEFUL HENRY

A Slow Drag

⑤

By Harry Kelly

Published by CARL HOFFMAN MUSIC CO.
KANSAS CITY. MO.

146

PEACEFUL HENRY.
(A Slow Drag.)

By E. H. KELLY.

✱ If the Octaves are too difficult use the lower notes.

Copyright 1901 by Carl Hoffman Music Co.

TRIO.

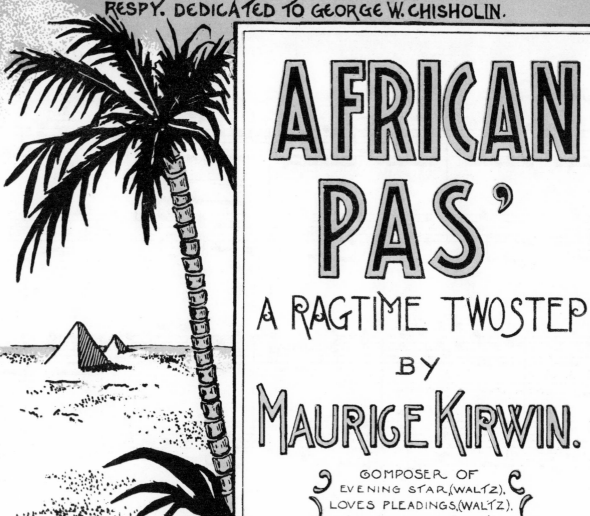

AFRICAN PAS'

A RAGTIME TWOSTEP

BY

MAURICE KIRWIN.

COMPOSER OF
EVENING STAR, (WALTZ).
LOVES PLEADINGS, (WALTZ).
LIGHT OF HOPE, (WALTZ).
VILLAGE CHIMES, (CAPRICE).
AMERICAN GUARDS, (MARCH).

John Stark & Son
SHEET MUSIC PUBLISHERS
St. Louis

AFRICAN PAS'.

RAG TIME TWO-STEP.

Composed by
MAURICE KIRWIN.

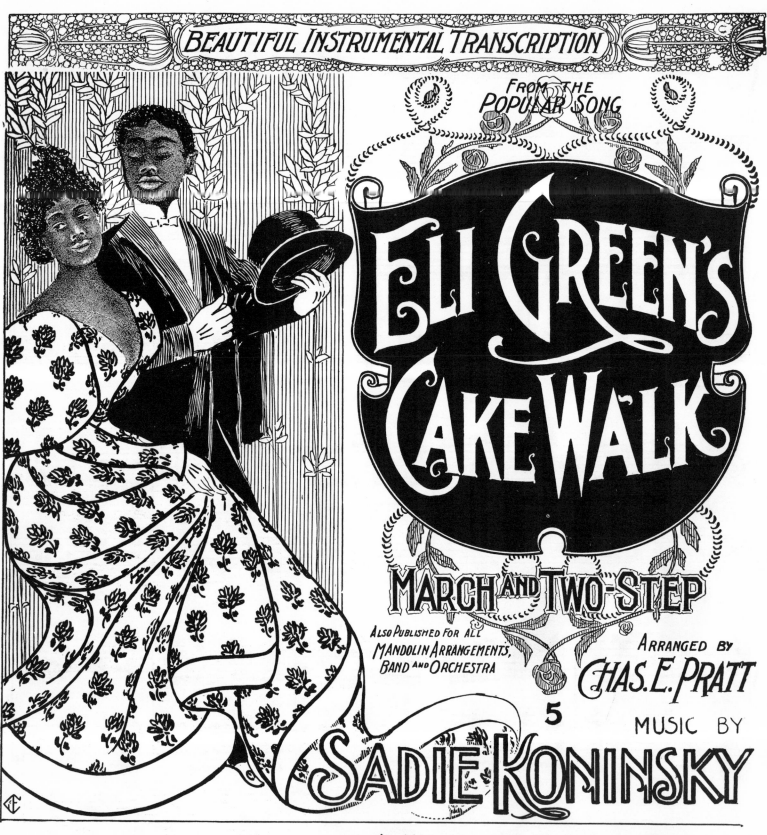

BEAUTIFUL INSTRUMENTAL TRANSCRIPTION

FROM THE POPULAR SONG

ELI GREEN'S CAKE WALK

MARCH AND TWO-STEP

ALSO PUBLISHED FOR ALL MANDOLIN ARRANGEMENTS, BAND AND ORCHESTRA

ARRANGED BY CHAS. E. PRATT

5

MUSIC BY SADIE KONINSKY

"THE HOUSE OF HITS" (TRADE MARK) REG. 1899. Published by JOS. W. STERN & CO. 34 East 21st St., NEW YORK MARK STERN BUILDING — NEW YORK, CHICAGO AND LONDON

LONDON. JOS. W. STERN & CO.
SOLE AGENTS FRANK DEAN & CO., 31 CASTLE ST. LONDON.

BANJO SOLO.
BANJO AND PIANO.

MEDLEY WALTZ.
GUITAR SOLO.

——— ALSO PUBLISHED FOR ———

All Mandolin and Guitar Arrangements, Zither, Quartette, Full Orchestra and Band

ELI GREEN'S CAKE WALK.

(Instrumental.)

CHARACTERISTIC MARCH.

By Sadie Koninsky.

157

TRIO.

TO COMUS CLUB. CHICAGO.

SHAKE YO' DUSTERS
OR
PICCANINNY RAG

TWO STEP.
BY

SONG .40   TWO-STEP .50

W. H. KRELL,
AUTHOR OF

"THE MISSISSIPPI RAG."   "DREAM OF THE BALL WALTZES."   "FIRST EXTRA WALTZES."   "ARBUTUS WALTZ."
"SUMMER GIRL WALTZES." & "TIME HE LOVES THE BEST WALTZ."

COPYRIGHT SECURED IN ENGLAND.

Published by
THE S. BRAINARD'S SONS CO.
CHICAGO.

ALL RIGHTS RESERVED.

Copyright MDCCCXCVIII., by The S. Brainard Sons Co.

CHAS. SHEARD & CO., 192 High Holborn, London.

SHAKE YO' DUSTERS!

OR

PICCANINNY RAG
TWO-STEP.

W. H. KRELL.

feels mighty proud and ma heart does beat, When dat Pic- ca- nin- ny shakes his   feet.

BY THE COMPOSER OF TEMPTATION RAG

SURE FIRE RAG

BY HENRY E. LODGE

VICTOR KREMER CO. CHICAGO NEW YORK LONDON SYDNEY

SURE FIRE RAG.

By HENRY LODGE.
Composer of "TEMPTATION RAG."

FELIX RAG

BY

H.H. McSKIMMING

A Phenomenal
Double Ragtime
Two-Step

PUBLISHED BY
H.H. McSKIMMING PUB. Co.
KIOWA,   KANS.

FELIX RAG.

H. H. Mc SKIMMING.

Moderato.

H.S.Talbot & Co.
Music Print Chicago.

IMPECUNIOUS DAVIS

CHARACTERISTIC Two-Step March, Polka & Cake-Walk.

BY KERRY MILLS

COMPOSER OF
"RASTUS ON PARADE."
"HAPPY DAYS IN DIXIE."
"AT A GEORGIA CAMPMEETING
"WHISTLING RUFUS."

F.A.Mills
MUSIC PUBLISHER
NEW YORK
43 WEST 29TH STREET.
CHICAGO,
CENTRAL MUSIC HALL BUILD.
COR. STATE & RANDOLPH STS.

5

IMPECUNIOUS DAVIS.

Characteristic Two–step, March and Cake–walk.

By KERRY MILLS.

Composer of { "Rastus on Parade," "Happy Days in Dixie," "At a Georgia Camp-meeting," "Whistling Rufus!" }

NOTE.—Davis lived in Black Creek, a small town on the Mississippi, just north of New Orleans. He was never known to have earned anything, and depended entirely upon the charitableness of the surrounding inhabitants for his existence; in fact, he considered that he was a child of Nature, and that the World owed him a living.

The white folks called him "IMPECUNIOUS DAVIS."

In a peculiarly contented and happy-go-lucky way he would lounge around the levees for hours at a time, humming quaint, weird, haunting melodies; some of these had a patriotic flavor, which was probably due to his living at the time of the war of the Rebellion.

The composer takes this opportunity of portraying the musical eccentricities of IMPECUN--IOUS DAVIS.

TRIO.

 FAVORITES

PRICE, 50 CENTS EACH.

Ray Lewis

311

PUBLISHED BY
PIONEER MUSIC PUBLISHING COMPANY
315 Dearborn Street, CHICAGO.

Glad Cat Rag.

by WILL NASH.

TRIO.

p dolce.

a la Cadenza.

LOUISIANA.

RAG TWO-STEP.

Composed by THEO. H. NORTHRUP.

Cocoanuts.

If this arrangement is too difficult, try the simplified arrangement on last page.

* Cocoanuts.

FINE.

LOUISIANA RAG. TWO-STEP.

SIMPLIFIED.

THEO. H. NORTHRUP.

192 · *Theodore H. Northrup*

Rag Pickers Rag

Two Step

Eversman Photo

COMPOSED BY

Robt. J. O'Brien

PUBLISHED BY

The Union Music Co.

Cincinnatus Bldg. Cincinnati O.

Eastern Agents

ENTERPRISE MUSIC SUPPLY CO

42 WEST 28th St. NEW YORK

Whaley Royce & Co | Hopwood & Carew
Toronto Canada. | London Eng.

NEW YORK ENGRAVING CO CIN T.O

The Rag Pickers Rag.

ROBT. J. O'BRIEN.

Trio.

MAJESTIC RAG

By

Ben Rawls

and

Royal Neel

TO

Scott Birdsong

5

PUBLISHED BY
BUSH AND GERTS
DALLAS   TEXAS

MAJESTIC RAG

BEN RAWLS
&
ROYAL NEEL

INTRO.
Not too fast

Cole Smoak
By
Clarence H St. John
"Ragtime Bob" DARCH
P.O. BOX 323, VIRGINIA CITY, NEV.
Found 1957 - St. Louis Mo.
PUBLISHERS OF
RAG TIME THAT IS DIFFERENT
STARK MUSIC CO.
ST. LOUIS, MO.
127 EAST 23 ST.
NEW YORK
W M YOUNG
5

"COLE SMOAK"
Rag.

By CLARENCE H. ST. JOHN.

Not too fast.

Trio.

A Summer Breeze

March and Two Step

By

JAMES SCOTT

James Scott

Published by
DUMARS MUSIC CO.
CARTHAGE, MO.

5

A Summer Breeze.

March and Two Step.

JAMES SCOTT.

* If the octaves are too difficult play the lower notes.

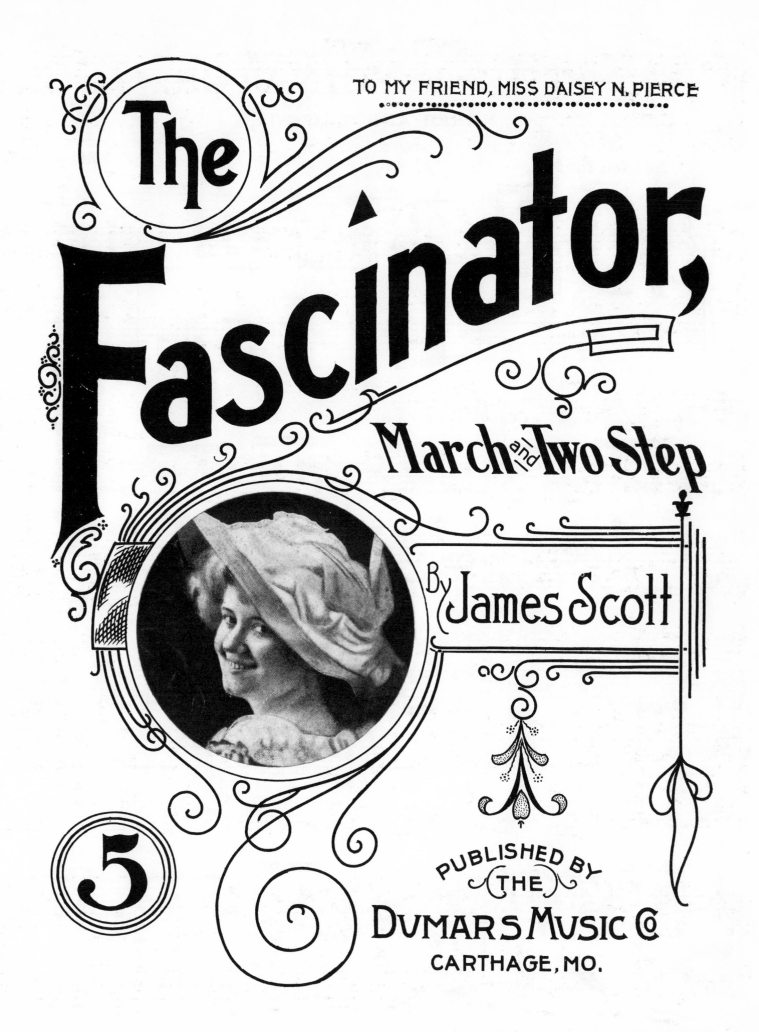

To my friend, Miss Daisy N. Pierce.

THE FASCINATOR.

MARCH AND TWO-STEP.

JAMES SCOTT.

Especially dedicated to the Visitors of the Pike.

ON THE PIKE.
(A Rag-time Two-Step.)

JAMES SCOTT.

Not too fast.

TRIO. *Repeat 8va.*

Jungle Time

A Genuine Rag

By E. Philip Severin

PUBLISHED BY

E. P. SEVERIN
Music Company.

1124-4TH AVE.
MOLINE-ILL.

HITS-THAT ARE REAL-ITS

5

JUNGLE TIME.
A GENUINE RAG.

E. PHILIP SEVERIN.
Composer of the famous
"PEANUTS FROLIC TWO STEP."

X. L. RAG

March Two-Step

Composed by

L. EDGAR SETTLE

35

SEDALIA, MO.:
Published by A. W. PERRY'S SONS, Music Publishers.

X. L. RAG.

MARCH TWO-STEP.

FOR PIANO OR ORGAN.

Composed by L. EDGAR SETTLE.

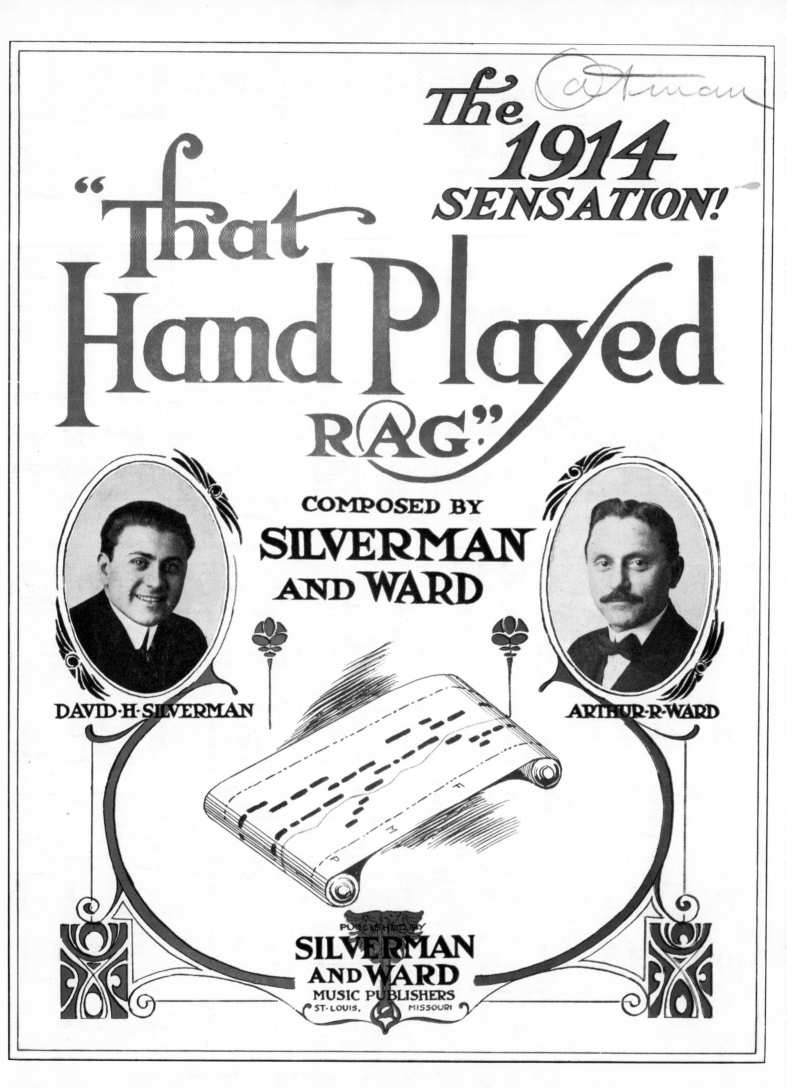

That "Hand-played" Rag.

By Silverman and Ward.

SPONGE

TWO STEP,

COMPOSED BY

W. C. SIMON

PUBLISHED BY W.C. SIMON
733 CANAL ST.
NEW ORLEANS, LA.

SPONGE

W. C. SIMON.

Moderato

238

SALLEE

KONETCHY

HUGGINS

HAUSER

MOWREY

G. LAUDERMILK

HARMON

L. LAUDERMILK

The CLIMBERS RAG

By — ARTHUR SIZEMORE

STEELE

BLISS

GOLDEN

Publishers
STARK MUSIC CO
3818 Laclede Ave St. Louis.

BRESNAHAN

⑤

SMITH

GEYER

ELLIS

OAKES

EVANS

McIVER

MAGEE

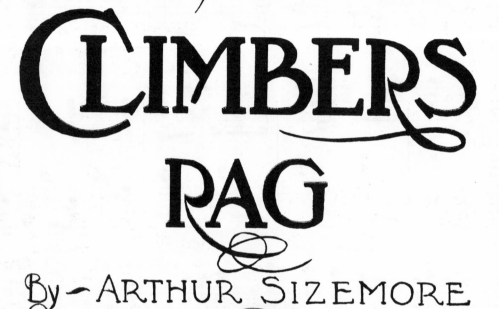

THE CLIMBERS

RAG.

ARTHUR SIZEMORE.
Composer
Blue Blazes Rag, etc.

NOTE: *Do not play this piece fast. It is never right to play "Ragtime" fast.*
Composer.

Tempo di drag.

Chloe Williams
BY RUSSELL SMITH
That Exponent of rag time
Writer of THE PRINCESS RAG
MICROBE RAG etc., etc.,
THAT
DEMON RAG
The J. Seidel Music Publishing Co.
INDIANAPOLIS, IND.
LOCK BOX 83
I. SEIDEL
E. SEIDEL

That Demon Rag.

RUSSELL SMITH.
Writer of "The Princess" "Microbe Rag" etc.

247

Toronto, Canada,
Whaley, Royce & Co.

PUBLISHED BY
Whitney-Warner Publishing Co.
Detroit, Mich.

London, W. C. Eng.
Chas. Sheard & Co.

"Ma Rag Time Baby."

(Two Step.)

FRED. S. STONE.

THE WATERMELON TRUST.
A SLOW DRAG.

by Harry C. Thompson.
Composer of A Black Bawl.

Moestoso.

TRIO.

A Cotton Patch Ragtime Two Step.

BY
CHARLES A. TYLER
King of Ragtime Composers.

Piano	50
Mandolin and Guitar	50
Two Mandolins and Guitar	60
Mandolin & Piano	60
Two Mandolins and Piano	70
Band	50
Orchestra	75

KANSAS CITY MO.
J.W. JENKINS' SONS MUSIC CO.
Publishers.

A COTTON PATCH.
RAGTIME TWO STEP.

CHAS. A. TYLER.

Tempo Mod *to.*

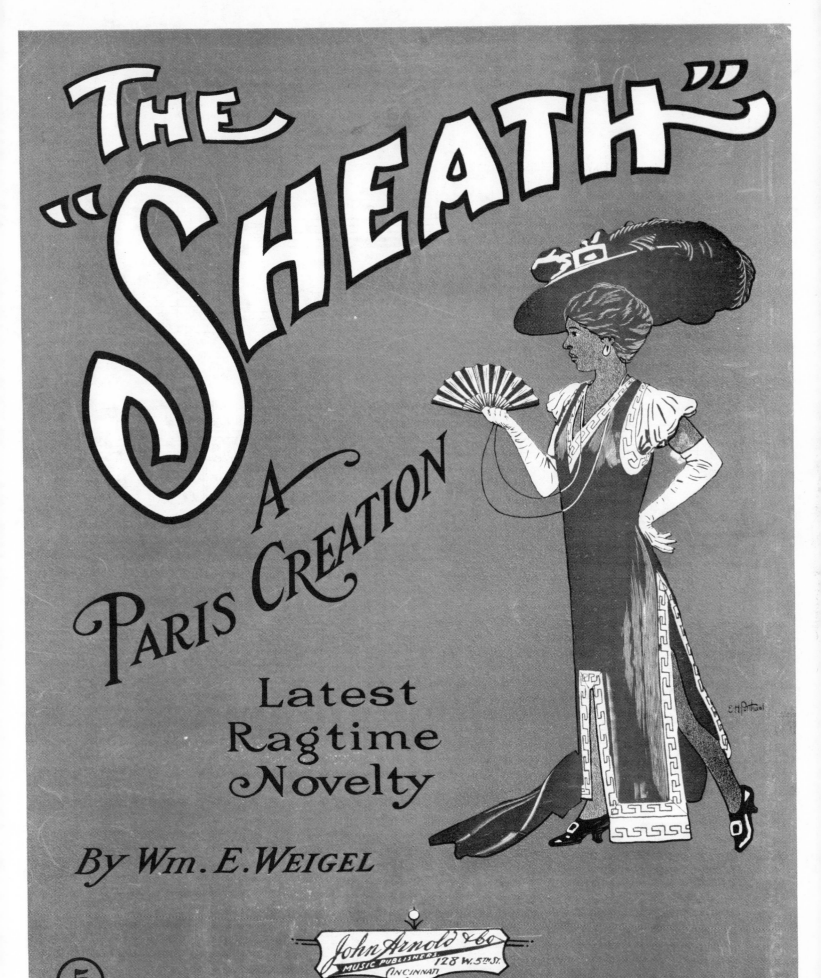

"The Sheath"
A Ragtime Two Step

W. E. WEIGEL

Introduction

Piano

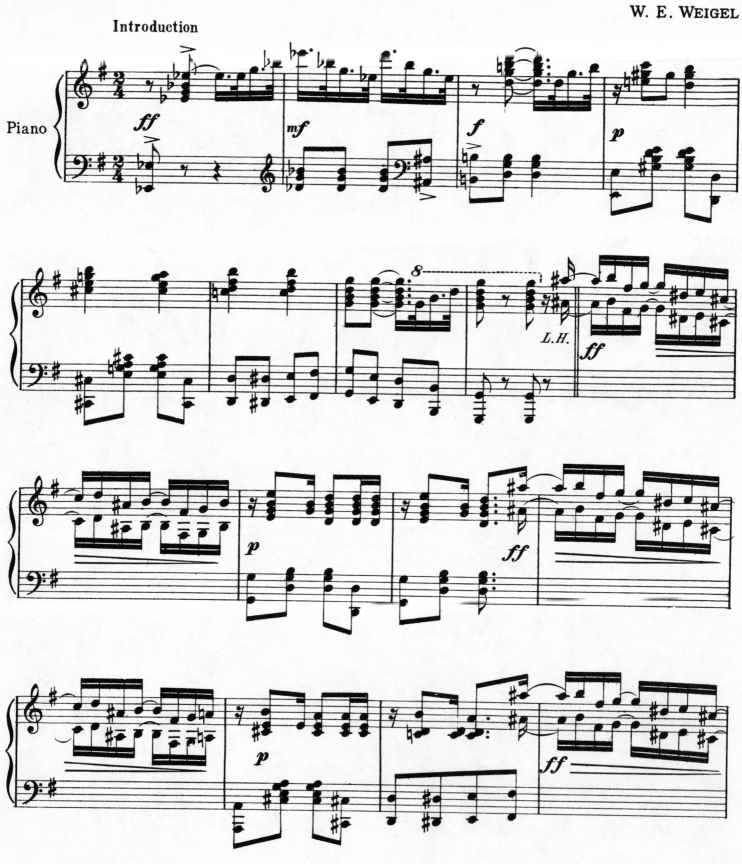

Peaches and Cream.

PERCY WENRICH.
Composer of "Mexicana."

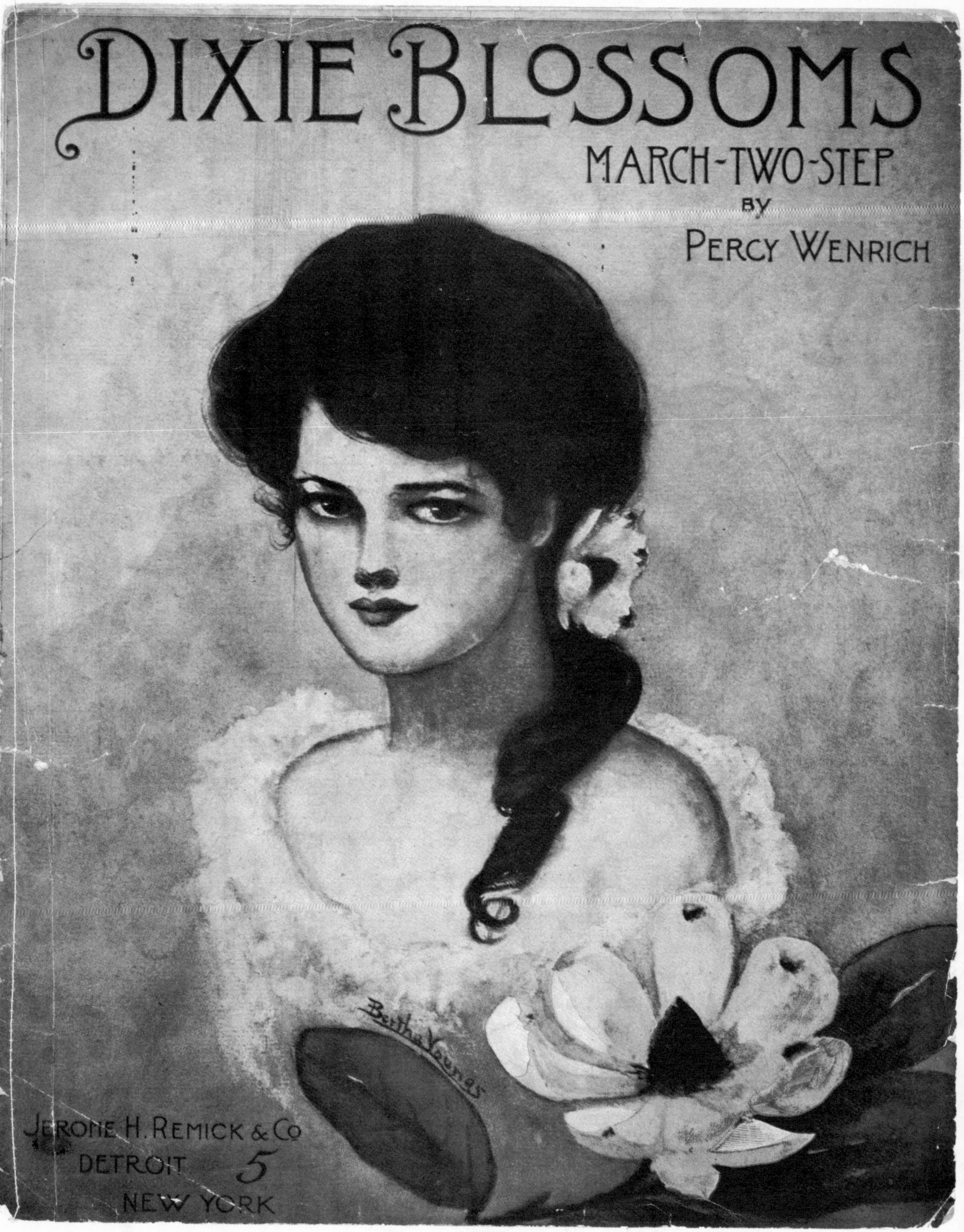

DIXIE BLOSSOMS

MARCH-TWO-STEP

BY

PERCY WENRICH

JEROME H. REMICK & CO
DETROIT 5
NEW YORK

To my sister Miss Nellie Wenrich

Dixie Blossoms.
TWO-STEP.

PERCY WENRICH.

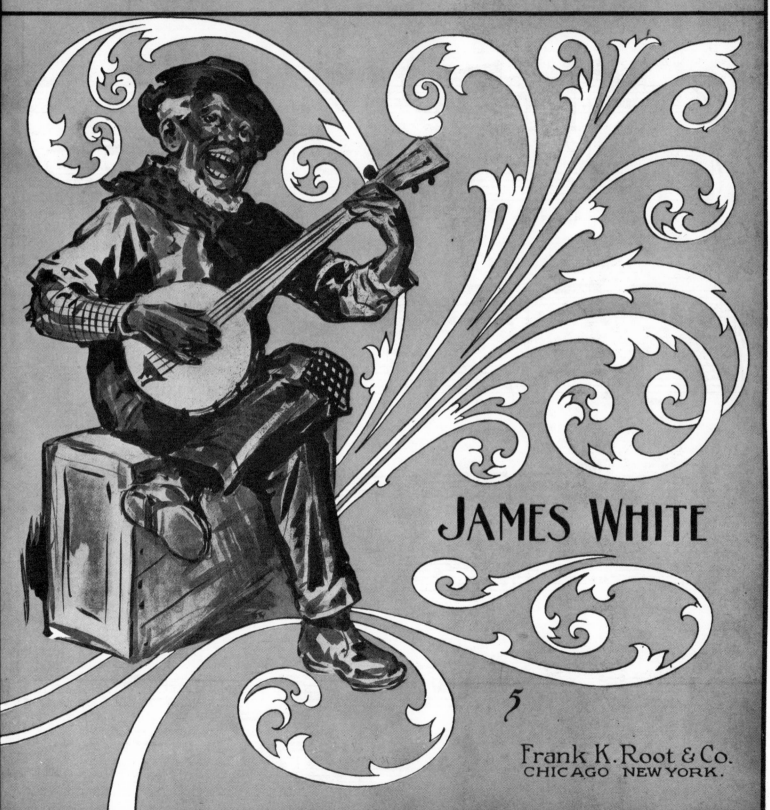

The Original
CHICAGO BLUES

JAMES WHITE

Tempo di Blues

CAR-BARLICK-ACID

RAG-TIME

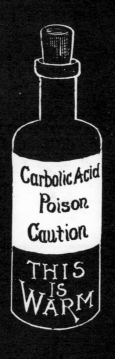

Something New in Rag-Time

A HOT PIECE OF RAG-TIME

COMPOSED BY

CLARENCE C. WILEY.

Oskaloosa, Iowa

An Excellent Piano Piece for Rag-time Lovers
Also a Fine Two-Step and Cake Walk

5

Published and Copyrighted by Clarence C. Wiley Oskaloosa, Iowa.

"CAR - BARLICK - ACID."

TWO - STEP - CAKE WALK.

Composed by CLARENCE WILEY.

THE QUEEN RAG.

AS PLAYED ON THE STEAMER "ISLAND QUEEN".

MARCH AND TWO STEP

BY FLOYD WILLIS

COMPOSER OF

"RAGGY" RAG." "WATERMELON MOSE".

"KENTUCKY" RAG, "RAVLINS" ETC.

6   6

FROM THE HOUSE OF
→KROLAGE←
THE JOS. KROLAGE MUSIC PUBLISHING CO.
S.E. COR. RACE AND ARCADE   CINCINNATI. O.

THE QUEEN RAG

TWO STEP

FLOYD WILLIS

Composer of

{ Raggy Rag
Kentucky Rag
Ravlins
Water Melon Mose etc }

287

TRIO

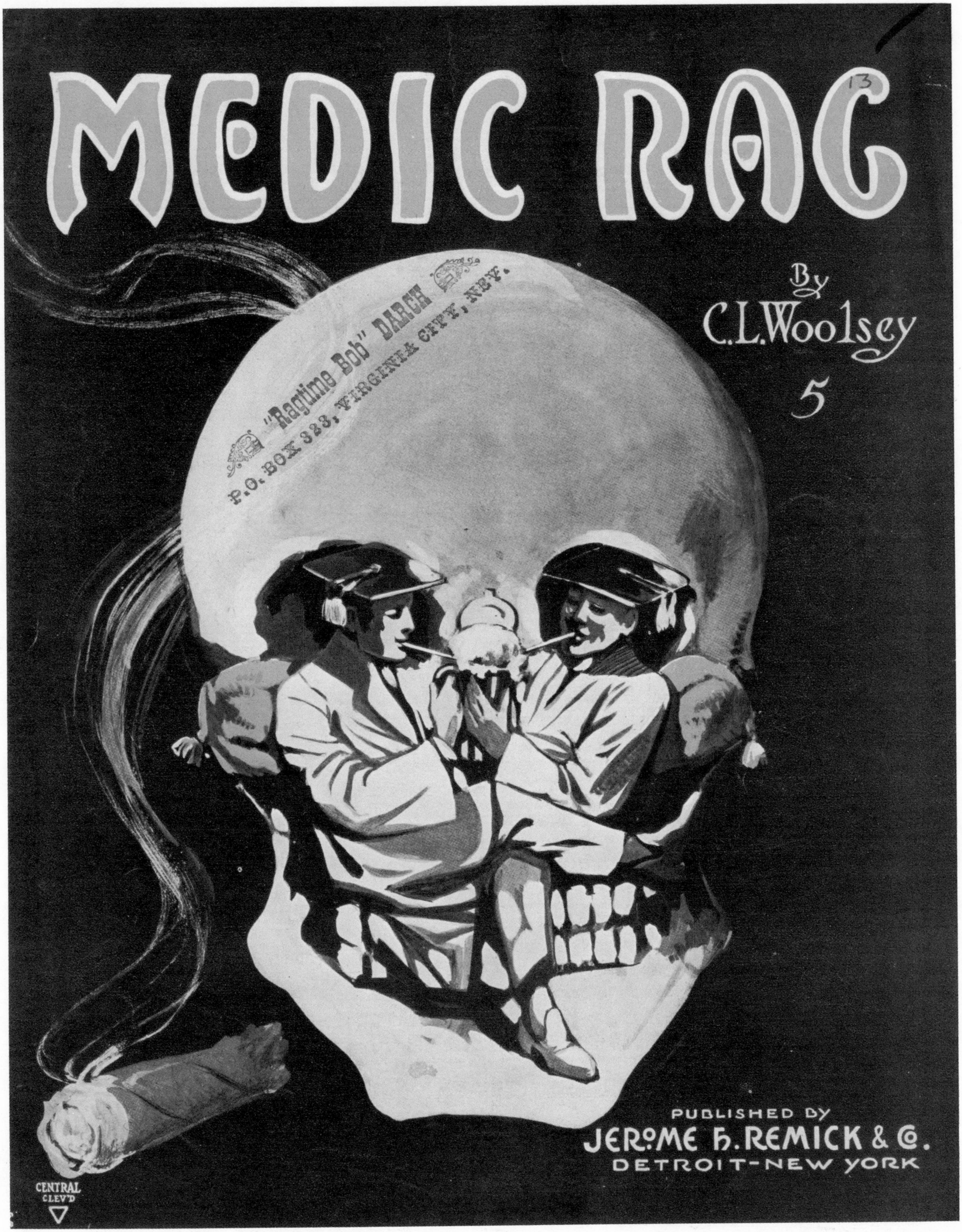
MEDIC RAG
By
C.L.Woolsey
5
"Ragtime Bob" DARCH
P.O. BOX 323, VIRGINIA CITY, NEV.
PUBLISHED BY
JEROME H. REMICK & CO.
DETROIT-NEW YORK
CENTRAL
CLEV'D

"MEDIC RAG"

Ragtime Two-Step.

C. L. WOOLSEY.

Tempo di rag.

TRIO.

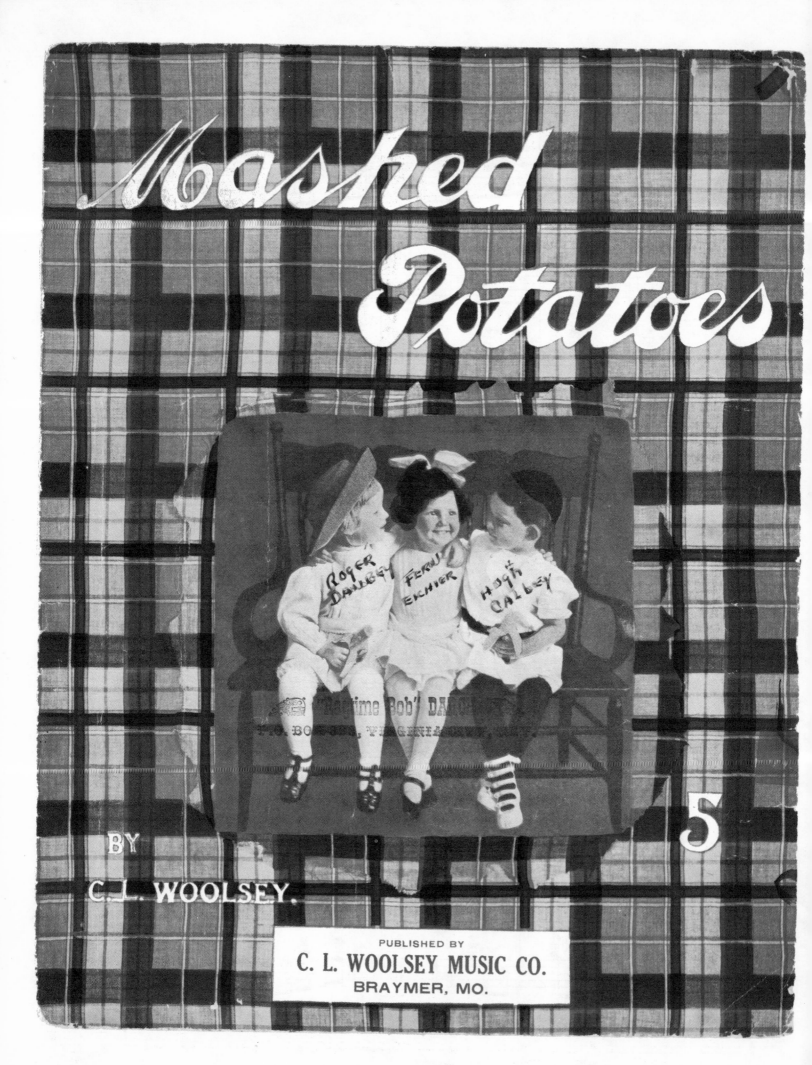

"MASHED POTATOES"

C. L. WOOLSEY.

297

The Black Cat Rag.

March & Two Step.

FRANK WOOSTER & ETHYL B. SMITH.

INDEX OF TITLES